TRANSITIONING TO
VIRTUAL
AND
HYBRID
EVENTS

BEN CHODOR
WITH GABRIELLA CYRANSKI

TRANSITIONING TO

VIRTUAL

AND

HYBRID

EVENTS

HOW TO CREATE, ADAPT, AND MARKET
AN **ENGAGING ONLINE EXPERIENCE**

WILEY

Library of Congress Cataloging-in-Publication Data is Available:

ISBN 9781119747178 (Hardcover)
ISBN 9781119747192 (ePDF)
ISBN 9781119747185 (ePub)

Cover Design: Wiley
Cover Image: icons © Bakai/Getty Images
Author Photo: © INTRADO DIGITAL MEDIA

Printed in the United States of America

SKY10020625_082120

This book is dedicated to all the dreamers who never let the world put them in a box!

I need to thank Sam Gilbert for being the first person who believed in me at 16. Marvin Share, who gave me incredible advice when I was just starting my journey as an adult, and Lee Perlman, who thought my first streaming idea was worth funding. Perry Shelman, who believed in me enough to help change my life forever, and Drew VanVooren, a true visionary, who was taken from this world way too soon and believed in me from the moment we met and whom I had the privilege of calling a friend and partner. John Shlonsky, Matt Nord, Robert Kaslow-Ramos, and Apollo Global Management, who entrusted me with the keys to build, grow, and dominate at Intrado, and the entire Intrado Digital Media team, whom I go to bed every night hoping I did right by. Gabriella Cyranski, who tirelessly worked on this book with me; without her we would not have made our deadline: you are so talented, and it was an honor to do this with you!

Most importantly my ride-or-die partner for life, my wife, Julie, and my inspirations, Rachel and Zachary, who taught me what unconditional love means.

Also, a special thanks to Dan Lotzof, Kathleen Alcorn, Scott Farb, Malcolm Lotzof, Lisa Davis, Erik Carlson, Simon Ball, Nancy Disman, John Whalen, Spiro Yulis, Dan Rehal, Mike McCauley, Bob Spass, Steve Manket, Sylvie Harton, Keith Barrett, Jim Phalen, Angelo Alduino, Adam Cohen, Christina Guthrie, and Michael Campbell.

CONTENTS

FOREWORD

If you are reading this book, you are interested in either running your first virtual event or taking your existing virtual events to a new level. In either case, you have come to the right place.

There is no question that today with the physical event world temporarily ceasing to exist as a result of regional lockdowns from COVID-19, the world of virtual events is thriving. However, virtual events themselves are not new. As CEO of INXPO, now part of Intrado, the leading online event platform, Ben and I have been delivering virtual events since 2004.

I originally met Ben, who at the time was CEO of Stream57, the leading video streaming platform, in early 2005. Even at that time we were both passionate believers that video delivered over the Internet was about to disrupt the event business. Ben was focused on video capture and streaming while we were focused on how to put a full event online. Combining our virtual event platform together with Ben's streaming services and technology, we have delivered some of the earliest high-performing interactive virtual events for some of the world's largest organizations and have been doing so for over 15 years.

Since that time, Ben and I have collaborated on multiple projects culminating in the sale of our company, INXPO, to Ben, who is currently president of Intrado Digital Media. My respect for Ben's understanding of this space, and his passion for disruption in this space, goes without saying. Ben is also the consummate technology leader. His focus on positivity, humility, and honesty makes him a leader that people trust and follow, allowing him to have successfully built multiple technology companies.

If you are in the market to host a virtual event, there is no better source of information available to you than this book. It is based on many years of practical hard-earned experience. Just because an event is online does not mean it's a no brainer to produce. Many components like organizing content, driving an audience, registration, and driving outcomes are the same in both physical and virtual events. However, technology plays a much larger role on the virtual side.

By reading this book you will have a much better appreciation for all the intricacies of hosting a successful virtual event. Your knowledge level will increase dramatically without ever having hosted your own virtual event, courtesy of Ben's hard-earned experiences.

–Malcolm Lotzof

INTRODUCTION

I have been in the digital media space since 1999, and I now have the honor of leading 1,300 global professionals at Intrado Digital Media, where we are working with over 13,000 clients around the world helping them deliver mission-critical communications to their employees, customers, media, and investors. I have always believed that virtual events add to any physical event and that all organizations should be taking most of their events hybrid; to me it's all about reaching your audience wherever they are, and on any device they choose.

So, let's get one thing straight: **Virtual events do not cannibalize physical events;** the world is what cannibalizes physical events. If you create meaningful and engaging virtual events, they're going to drive your audience to want to be there physically if they can.

I have had the honor to work with some of the most recognizable brands in the world and some of the most talented and creative people. We've helped an incredible number of organizations make the leap into the world of virtual events. Throughout this book we will not only tell you about going virtual, we will give you the tools and know-how to help make your move into this exciting world that is needed now more than ever before. For those of you already creating virtual events we will give you some insight on what works and doesn't work, as well as plenty of checklists, best practices, and tips; consider this book your virtual events playbook!

Let's start with my journey into this world of streaming, hybrid, and virtual events so I can show you why I'm the guy that can successfully guide you through *your* virtual event journey.

My first hybrid event was for a major designer's fashion show at Grand Central Terminal in New York, where there was physical audience and a virtual audience.

The ask from this client was: How do you take the intimacy of a fashion show, with models walking down a runway, and make it exciting for the journalists, buyers, and customers who could not make it to NYC for Fashion Week and secure the hard-to-get ticket?

We were able to do this by giving the virtual audience the best seat in the house and incredible camera angles, but the key element was giving this audience more, which included a behind-the-scenes look at what goes on backstage to put on a fashion show. They were able to actually ask a designer questions before the show, and as a little sneak peek, the virtual attendees saw the new fashions a few moments before the actual live attendees did.

My second hybrid event that we produced was for one of the most successful rock bands of all time. Their ask was: How do we not only make the virtual audience feel like they are at the concert, but allow them to be the director of their version of the show wherever they were watching the concert?

This event was taking place at the then-named Garden State Art Center in Holmdel, New Jersey, with 10,000-plus screaming fans at the venue and tens of thousands watching via web who we not only gave the concert experience to but also allowed them to get involved in the show. In short, we got creative and this is how we did it:

1. We had a typical concert five-camera production setup, with a camera set up for wide shots so you could see the entire band. There was another camera set up so you could see the lead singer, and an overhead camera so you could see the whole band from above. Lastly, we had an additional camera focused on the audience and a final mobile camera so you could get various closeups on stage.

2. To get creative we decided to give the virtual audience control of their camera views and also added three more lipstick cameras (they are called lipstick cameras because they are the size of a lipstick) so we could put one on the lead

singer's microphone, put one around the neck of the drummer, and the last on the hat of the lead guitarist. While you were watching virtually you could either watch a mixed program feed that we directed or at any time you could click to the view that you wanted. Giving the controls to the audience gave them the ability to not only watch the concert but see the concert the way they wanted to.

3. We set up a pre-concert virtual meet-and-greet with the band, where a few lucky virtual attendees got to ask the band questions before the concert.

4. We also enabled one lucky virtual attendee to request a song that the band would play at this concert.

End result, the virtual audience had a unique experience that they would not have had at the live concert.

Now let's fast-forward to today and the reasons that have brought you to pick up this book. Where were you when the world changed forever and got you to this point? The point where virtual and hybrid events became a necessity in not only your event strategy but your overall business strategy.

I was just getting back from our sales kickoff world tour. We started in New York and then went to Chicago; Los Angeles; Toronto; London; France; Malmo, Sweden; and our last location was Sydney, Australia. We flew home on a Thursday. On the following Monday I was asked to join a call with one of the largest online retailers in the world for their Entrepreneurial Fund event, where they were going to give $5 million in investment funding to the winners. They had decided to cancel their physical event in China because of the risk COVID-19 was posing to the world. In under 11 business days we created their first-ever virtual event, where they had over 45 presenters from all over the world who could not make the trip to China, or were downright prohibited from making it. Little did we know when we were helping them move this incredible event from a physical event to virtual event that this would be the start of a global movement that would take us from interacting in person with business associates and friends at physical events to a world of work from home, videoconferences, and 100% virtual events.

I haven't looked back since, and I expect virtual will remain a highly valuable channel for our future and a driver of revenue and profit growth, but success will depend on delivering truly innovative programs that educate and inspire your audiences and deliver meaningful and measurable ROI to customers and sponsors.

This book, your virtual events playbook, will give you the knowledge you need to navigate this new world of virtual events and to plan and execute a successful virtual event strategy! I tapped into some of the most knowledgeable professionals I know in the world of broadcast television, streaming, event production, design, and marketing and asked them for their secrets on how to make the leap into virtual events. I have incorporated these tips into this book; I cannot thank them enough for the invaluable input. I am excited that you picked this book to help you on your journey into the incredible world of virtual events and remember when reading it that this is your journey and you have to add your own creativity and look at this adventure as a blank canvas to create something memorable. I cannot wait to participate in one of your events!

CHAPTER 1

Understanding Virtual and Hybrid Events

The nature of events has changed forever. Companies are reconsidering their in-person event strategies and shifting to virtual or hybrid events instead.

A little fact that I found in a recent survey conducted in early 2020 was that 78% of marketing leaders said they expected to significantly increase their budgets when it came to virtual events. That says it all; the need for virtual events continues to grow so if you understand and master them, you'll position yourself as a forward-thinking asset in your organization.

You can't just take a physical event, make it virtual, and instantly expect the attendees to have an incredible user experience, or expect your speakers to be able to make an easy transition to virtual when they won't be able to look into the eyes of the attendees, know if their jokes went over well, or hear their applause. But don't worry, by the time you finish reading this book, I promise you will have all the information you need to produce a virtual or hybrid event.

In this chapter, you'll get a basic understanding of virtual and hybrid events, including benefits and challenges, and I will also clear up some common myths and misconceptions about taking your events virtual.

GOING VIRTUAL

A virtual event is a meeting or conference that either was originally held as a physical event and moved to be online or was created to exist only online. The only way that you can access and attend the event is via the internet from a computer, laptop, mobile device, or OTT (over the top) on a Smart TV.

Enterprise companies have been pushed to come up with new and innovative ways to connect with their customers, partners, and prospects. For years, large physical events have been a great way to network with these audiences and share new innovations, products, and services. Today, organizations have to turn to 100% virtual or hybrid events to extend the reach of their content, attract more interest in their company, and stay in touch with their investors, members, partners, and employees. The rapidly evolving event technology space has enabled companies to have thousands of additional people engage with a virtual event and keep them coming back to view on-demand after the event has ended. So instead of being at a physical event they are now participating from their home or office from any corner of the world.

A major benefit of the hiatus from in-person event delivery is that it has forced in-person events teams to finally embrace virtual delivery in ways that would not have been possible if they'd been focused on the production cycle of in-person events. Out of this hiatus has come an intense focus on how to integrate digital delivery of content: either as virtual-only or (in the future) as a mix of staged in-person and virtual delivery. The latter will be important because when in-person events do return, social distancing measures will continue to heavily impact the way events are staged, requiring larger space footprints to stage them, which will impact revenue and margins and can only be offset by the thoughtful integration of virtual delivery to enhance reach and drive ROI for sponsors.

Like most of us who were forced by COVID-19 to transition from in-person events to virtual-only and hybrid delivery models, you're going to learn a lot about this transition and the limitations of traditional program formats built around in-person attendees. What works for an in-person event does not necessarily translate to success online. You'll need to innovate and look at things differently, in terms of the types of content, the duration of sessions, and speaker and topic selection. Some considerations in this new virtual events world include:

- **Pre-Event Research:** gather questions to help shape the programs, and leverage integrated channel marketing to foster meaningful audience engagement.

- **Content Integration:** work to align content produced at virtual events within your year-round content strategy so you're able to continually nurture audiences.

- **Value of Curation:** analyze what is the best way to capture your content. You may find it's better to record sessions with certain speakers so you can spend the time after the content is recorded to edit and create a more dynamic presentation. However, other speakers may be better captured live.

NOTE

"As an information services company, we have recently invested significantly in our virtual events products and platform, because we understood the value and importance of the channel in distributing content to our most engaged audiences. An analysis of our audience data revealed that our virtual attendees are among our most loyal and engaged audiences, often spending hours consuming and interacting with our brands and branded content, all the while generating unique perspectives and insights on industry topics, products, or trends. In fact, most of our top customers have grown with us through deeper adoption of our virtual events platform."

—John Whelan, CEO of the Cyber Risk Alliance

You can leverage the brand trust that you've established among your attendees and customers to migrate them to virtual delivery in lieu of in-person delivery without impacting revenue.

Virtual event attendees are a rich source of data insight to build programs to deepen the relationship between your brand and customers. You can also use the insight to cultivate market and customer perspectives, which can allow you to significantly enhance the value of your marketing solutions.

Having established the strategic value of your virtual event audience, you can make them the focal point of your content and audience growth strategy, seeking to expand the range of content and programming on your virtual event platform, and to position interaction as a core component of your customer's journeys.

OPTING FOR A HYBRID EVENT

A *hybrid event* is a physical event that has a portion or the entire content program available online; bottom line, there is always a physical element to a hybrid event.

The obvious and immediate appeal is the expanded reach you have to engage a larger audience that doesn't attend the physical event. We know for the foreseeable future, events will be virtual and even when we go back to physical events you will still see a virtual/hybrid portion of the program included; the world has changed forever. Think of the hybrid element of your event as your event insurance policy going forward. It is your continuity plan in this unpredictable world we now live in. When I first got into the world of streaming and virtual events, a lot of event organizers would be worried that if they offered their event and programming online, that they would have fewer people attend the physical event because attendees would decide to stay home and watch online and they would make less money from the event.

I used to tell clients, prospects, and anyone who could hear my voice, that virtual events do not cannibalize physical events. In fact a good virtual event will make the virtual attendee want to attend physically and it would give you the ability to grow your audience and keep your event going after the physical event ended, but a lot of event planners were still too scared about the risk of cannibalization of their event and could not see the value of bringing their events virtual. Well guess what: it's not that virtual events are cannibalizing your physical events, it's that the world has now cannibalized your physical event.

Many forward-thinking companies have and will use hybrid events to increase their audience across geographical divides and further their education and communication. Despite fears of dropping in-person attendance, data suggests that physical face-to-face participation increases with hybrid events. Hybrid events also extend the reach and life of your content, allowing companies to tap into new markets, acquire new attendees/users, and open the doors to more business opportunities and engagements. As we think about going back to some sort of physical event, I believe you should add a virtual or hybrid element to any meeting or conference you are planning now or in the future; the technology is finally here to enable you to easily do it.

As I look to the future, I believe we will start with smaller physical events, let's say audience sizes up to 100 or so people meeting simultaneously in various cities around the country or even around the world at the same time, and you will be streaming/broadcasting to and from each of the locations and to a virtual audience, all at the same time. I believe even when you plan meetings with thousands of attendees, you will have satellite/hybrid audiences at various physical locations and a virtual audience participating from home or their offices.

LEVERAGING THE POWER OF VIDEO AT HYBRID EVENTS TO ENHANCE AUDIENCE ENGAGEMENT AND SATISFACTION

I have had the honor of working on a lot of truly innovative and amazing virtual and hybrid events, so I asked a former client and collaborator to give an example of one of his hybrid events from the pharmaceutical industry. This is a hybrid event that I had the privilege of working on with Spiro Yulis, CEO and Founder of SkyArx, a pharmaceutical and healthcare marketing and event company.

(continued)

(*continued*)

A global top 10 pharmaceutical company was launching a new respiratory product and wanted to include virtual events as part of its promotional strategy for communicating with health-care professionals. The marketing team had experienced limited success with traditional webcast programs for other product launches and was looking for a more innovative, engaging, and personal virtual solution.

After consulting with the client on a variety of approaches, they decided on the delivery of a hybrid solution broadcasting to live and virtual audiences.

The primary speaker for the series, an international thought leader in respiratory medicine, presented as part of a live dinner program in front of 75 physicians at a restaurant in a major market. His presentation was broadcast to audiences at 15 other live dinner programs across the U.S. as well as hundreds of at-home viewers.

We featured all these remote audiences across the country on-camera as part of the broadcast to create a sense of connectedness among participants and foster a more personal and engaging question-and-answer session. We also enabled audiences from their homes or offices to participate and ask questions as well.

Each live program site was staffed by a single-camera broadcast crew to capture audience activity that was integrated into the broadcast. The show opening included a "round robin" of live introductions of each location, where the local pharmaceutical representative program host shared a greeting from their audience with some local flare. Live footage from the sites was peppered in throughout the broadcast, with a fun and lively second screen gamification activity mid-program to keep the audience energized.

Participants from all sites were invited to ask the speaker questions live, on camera, at intervals during the broadcast,

(*continued*)

showing in split-screen with the presenter. Offering a real-time, on-camera, verbal exchange with this national thought leader was a big draw for them, and a differentiator from typical webcasts where audiences are limited to typing their questions into the perceived "great abyss" of a webcast platform, only for them to go unaddressed during – and after – the program. The "1:1" live interaction with the speaker and the ability for each of the live sites to see each other on camera were definite keys to success.

The final participant total (live and at-home) was a record for this company's virtual events in the respiratory category.

Results:

- Registration for the event was 77% higher than that for the company's previous product launch webcast. The program format created significant buzz with physicians, who then recruited colleagues, including some from practices previously flagged as inaccessible. The program also opened many doors for the sales team.

- 64% more participants joined this event than this marketing team's previous satellite national broadcast.

- In a post-event survey, 82% of participants reported that this was the most engaging hybrid virtual event in which they had participated. The real-time "face-to-face" interaction with the speaker and a feeling of connectedness with the other live sites were cited as the top two reasons.

- The company's leadership team was so pleased with the event and resulting product inquiries that they replicated this model across three following product launches.

Addressing Common Misconceptions and Myths about Virtual Events

When I started out in the streaming business in 1998, people still had fax machines, high-speed internet at home was a luxury and didn't exist in many locations, and streaming video was not HD quality and was the size of postage stamp and then a playing card. When you started a new job you probably got a desktop as opposed to a laptop computer. Oh, and to give you some context, the iPad was still 11 years away and the iPhone was still 9 years away. Also just to give more perspective, Joseph W. Lechleider, who is credited for being one of the inventors of high-speed internet, was probably never thinking about sending video over the internet; 4G internet was not launched in the United States until 2010. With 5G launching globally now, the ability to receive amazing quality content anywhere in the world is now well within reach.

In the early days of the internet, online events and webinars were a small part of the events business and, quite honestly, an afterthought for event planners and conference planners.

Cutting-edge advancements in video, audio, and integrated communication technologies have made it possible to do much more online. Gone are the days when companies were forced to deal with bulky, unintuitive webinar programs that produced poor-quality video or choppy, broken audio. Webcasting technology that unites high-quality, crystal-clear audio and video, PowerPoint, live chat, and Q&A into a single streamlined interface has removed technological barriers for large and small businesses. Now all you need is a strong internet connection and you can deliver a TV-style broadcast right from your home.

And with all these advancements, there is still a lot of resistance and uneasiness because of the misconceptions around virtual events.

Before we go any further in the book, I want to take you through all the myths you're going to hear and tell you exactly why they are not based in fact.

Myth #1: My virtual event or hybrid event will cannibalize my physical event attendance

Reality: I talked about this in earlier examples, but I'd like to give you another. A good friend of mine puts it like this: every year there are only about 70,000 total tickets to the Super Bowl. If I don't get a ticket, does that mean I'm not going to watch? Of course not; I'll watch but it will just be a different experience, and usually a cheaper one.

The reality doesn't support the cannibalization myth, but instead it shows how you should be thinking about the bigger picture. If you only offer an option to attend a physical event, you're leaving out a large segment of your prospect universe that won't get to see any of that content or engage with any of those attendees. You're missing an opportunity to extend your reach to a global audience that you were never in front of before.

For those determined to attend the physical event, your repeat customers, they fight each year for the travel and budget approval to see customers and partners face to face, and they're not going to give that up.

Myth #2: It can't be monetized, and I'll lose my sponsor and attendee revenue streams

Reality: Any good virtual event platform will have the option for you to collect attendee registration fees. Plus there are a number of customizable elements that can be monetized for exhibitors and sponsors to provide visibility, thought leadership opportunities, and custom messaging throughout the event experience. If it's customizable, it's monetizable.

Myth #3: It's not interactive; people will just be watching presentations

Reality: This couldn't be further from the truth. A virtual environment offers participants the option to participate in live polls during a session. Based on those poll results the speaker can pivot within the presentation to put more emphasis on areas of the topic attendees said they want to hear about.

Attendees can also take advantage of live chat, video chats, and Q&A. I've seen chat threads get really lively with people making connections, answering questions for one another, and offering their expertise on the topic. And lastly, you're able to pose questions directly to the speaker and get those answered in real time.

Myth #4: People won't stay as long for a virtual session as they would for an in-person session

Reality: It's just as easy to walk out of a physical session or not even show up to the meeting as it is to click out of a virtual event. I would argue that there are more distractions at a physical meeting where most are located in cities with great climates and an abundance of leisure activities. When you click out of a virtual event, you're just right back where you started from, at your desk.

Plus, in a virtual environment we can measure how long people stay within a session with more accuracy than a badge swipe so we can confidently tell you which sessions are the most popular.

Myth #5: I'll only get limited reporting

Reality: This one is always a bit of a shock to me because within a virtual environment, like everything we do online, there is always activity data being collected. Any virtual event platform that you choose should be able to provide you with enough data for marketing to develop a lead scoring model, for sponsors to know who visited their booths and what assets were downloaded, and for your executive leadership to be confident that the exact audience they targeted actually attended.

So now that you know what a virtual event is, it's time to introduce you to some of the innovative tools you can use in order to create a compelling virtual event.

CHAPTER 2

Understanding Virtual Communication Tools

S o, before we really dive into the playbook, I'll walk you through the difference between webinars, webcasts, streaming, virtual events, and web conferences and the best use cases for each. Each of these options can be part of your virtual event, but in order to have success with each option it needs to resonate with your audience and meet your business objectives.

Think about what you want to achieve with each program and your call to action for the participants desired. Is your goal to have them buy something, learn something, or engage with the program? Keep in mind the viewing habits of your audience: will they be watching from their computers, TVs, tablets, mobile devices, or potentially all of the above?

Also keep in mind you don't have to pick one; I am a big fan of using a blended mix of all the virtual tools at your disposal, because they all bring something unique in the way you get to deliver your message.

WEBINAR

A webinar is traditionally an audio-over-slide broadcast that includes Q&A and chat functionality. The presenter is not visible on-screen and the focus is on the slides using a microphone embedded directly in his or her computer or via a telephone connection. The virtual audience can type in questions and can also engage in open chat with a few viewers. Webinars are most commonly used for product launch or IT presentations where the focus is more on product specs or engineering details. These events are usually smaller in nature and may not always be available for on-demand. They can also be ideal for presenters who have low internet bandwidth that can't support video or do not want to be on-camera. Also, traditionally you would think of a webinar more as a seminar tool and one-way technology and not used for collaboration.

As well, one of the most attractive elements of a webinar is that that the software available to create webinars is fairly easy to use, the software is readily available, and they are a low-cost way of creating content and delivering it to your targeted audience.

Use Cases

Product Training - you launch a webinar series that will educate your channel partners about the technical details and functionality of a new product. You want to be able to have live Q&A available as well as open chat. You may not want the webinar to be available on-demand because of confidentiality issues.

Internal Communications - Your company introduces a brand-new expense tracking software that needs to roll out to regional employees over the course of a few weeks to educate and train as many employees as possible on detailed process flow. You need to focus on slides so employees can see how to go from one step to another. Because this is a training, you want to include audio over slides, Q&A, and a quiz at the end. In this use case it is important to have the program available on-demand so that your audience can take the learning course whenever they are available and not at a set time or day of the week.

WEBCASTING

A live webcast is an online broadcast that takes place at a specific date and time. Just like live television, a live webcast happens in real time, with no ability to edit or correct footage. The spontaneity of a live webcast is one reason users enjoy attending them. It is also my belief that one of the keys to a successful virtual event is not only the webcast's functionality but also the quality of your webcasts.

A live webcast may include one or more of these elements: slides, live video, Q&A, polls, surveys, online chat, and social media integration. Organizers of live webcasts choose which of these elements to include.

Live webcasts are streamed over the internet via webcam, professional and prosumer video equipment, broadcast studios, satellite feeds, or videoconference units from physical event locations, to your home, office, or any location that you can get an internet connection. End users can experience live webcasts from any internet connected device and in browsers or mobile apps. Today, 96% of consumers rely on a smartphone to get things done. That means you need to ensure your content is viewable on a small screen!

The newest webcasting technology provides a WebRTC presenter panel. WebRTC is an open source web and mobile technology that allows for real-time communications. What does that mean to your Webcast? It enables you to create a broadcast experience and bring other remote presenters into your webcast so that you can have real conversation live. This enables you to have a panel event or a one-on-one interview with each presenter in a different location. I have been streaming since the late 1990s and I think this is the biggest change and enhancement in the world of webcasting. It takes your webcast and turns it into a broadcast experience. My advice is when selecting a webcasting solution, make sure they have WebRTC presenter side capabilities. Speakers have access to a browser-based "presentation console" of live webcast platforms. This console provides controls that are available exclusively to presenters: starting and stopping the broadcast, advancing slides, viewing audience metrics, launching polls, viewing poll results, viewing questions, moderating questions, and more.

End users access the "audience console," which the live webcast platform makes available via browser or mobile app. The audience console enables users to view slides, hear audio, view video, participate in polls, submit questions, and access handouts.

An on-demand archive of the live webcast is available as soon as the live webcast is over. Users who missed the live broadcast can return later to watch the webcast on demand. The most common uses of webcasts are for employee town halls, marketing events, educational programs, and to broadcast from a hybrid event. One of my favorite parts of a webcast is that you can handle audiences of any size while also delivering a higher-quality program.

Going forward I think more and more physical events will also broadcast all or portions of their program to a virtual audience, creating a compelling hybrid viewing experience.

Note: The term "live webcast" is used synonymously with "live webinar" – just to clear up any confusion!

Use Cases

Corporate Announcement – Your CEO wants to address all of the employees with a quarterly town hall; some of the key elements are going to be an opening prerecorded video that the marketing team put together. Then the CEO will take the stage, and it could be his or her live video opening from an auditorium in front of employees at headquarters. After the opening, your CEO will incorporate slides and graphics to talk about quarterly results. The program will shift from graphics to one-on-one live interviews with a few key executives to congratulate them on their results, and to end the program there will be a panel of executives discussing the quarter, where they will take questions from employees. After the Q&A session is complete the webcast ends with a prerecorded montage of images of employees synced to music. The webcast can then be edited into smaller bitesize pieces of content to be shared internally or to the public. Also, this webcast can then be made available for employees to watch on-demand. Most webcasting solutions today offer you the ability to edit your content, or you can download the content and your internal or external production team can edit it themselves.

Marketing Thought Leadership – You are going to have two or three industry experts discuss a topic for 30 to 40 minutes and then take questions from the live virtual audience. The moderator will open the program and introduce the panelists, who would be in different locations. The key elements here are that all panelists are being broadcast via webcam video so the audience can see them and hear their interactions with the other panelists. This program could consist of some slides, software demos, and polling as well. The biggest difference between this and a webinar is the use of video and the ability to take portions of this webcast and repackage it to share key takeaways on your website or via social media.

STREAMING

Streaming is the term we will use for a broadcast that is going to Social Media locations like Facebook Live, YouTube, Twitch, Periscope/Twitter, LinkedIn Live, OTT channels like Roku's Smart TV and Apple TV, or imbedded into a company's website or partner's website. Streaming is ideally for syndicating your content live and on demand to various locations. It is a great way to broadcast your event. Additionally, all of the locations I mentioned above offer their own live streaming technology that you don't usually have to pay for, plus there are a lot of streaming services available for your organization to use. It feels like every day a new streaming service comes online and a new solution is available.

What is OTT, you might ask? OTT stands for "over the top." Traditionally, television was delivered via terrestrial broadcast and then moved to cable or satellite delivery. OTT is delivered directly to viewers via the internet, which is how all of the streaming networks are now delivered; think Netflix, Amazon, and Hulu to name a few.

You might be wondering why is it important for you to understand and know about OTT? It's because just like with virtual events and webcasting it is another avenue you might think of for delivering your event programing, and you now can integrate OTT programming in your virtual events. In other words, I can see the day when all associations, universities, and corporations have their own OTT channels in places like Apple TV, Roku, and Smart TVs, where the audience will go to get news and information from your organization, directly on their TV sets and conference room monitors. Your content can be delivered to any Smart TV or OTT device anywhere in the world. So technically anyone in the world could have access to your content if available on 50″, 60″, and larger television monitors with a click of their remote controls.

Use Cases

Marketing – A major announcement where your number-one goal is to reach as many people as possible. You care more about the mass numbers you reach than actually knowing who is watching – think television. You want to make it easy for the audience to log in from anywhere. Instead of making the audience come to your destination and registering, you're bringing your content to the places that your audience likes to get their content. And you're not limited to one: you can syndicate your content to many locations at once, like Facebook Live, LinkedIn Live, Twitch, your partners' websites, etc. You're hoping that they will like what they see and then come to your website to engage or purchase.

Corporate Television – You're a large association and you want to create your own TV channel to launch at your annual event and run all year round with new programming segments broadcast multiple times a week. Your first program can be viewed by the audience live at the conference, on a hotel TV channel, and on conference monitors; their virtual audience could watch the content via the association's website, a virtual event platform, and via your very own Roku channel. Your goal is to debut your program everywhere your audience wants to watch and drive them to continue to get similar programming through your TV channel 24/7 and 365 days a year.

WEB CONFERENCING

Web conferencing is a collaboration tool; it is a many-to-many solution – think of products like Zoom, Webex, BlueJeans, Hoot, and a whole host of others. These are perfect solutions for internal meetings and customer-facing product demos where you connect through your computer and activate your webcam so everyone can see each other and share your computer screen. You will normally purchase web conferencing technology on a license either annually for your entire organization or monthly for individual users or for small companies and start-ups. Also, unlike webcasting, webinars, and virtual events, you have one link that is dedicated to an individual, which is your web conference ID. This is a lower-cost way that you could accomplish the same goal as a webcast or webinar, but you do not have all the functionality like polls and surveys and you will also be limited to how many users can be on your conferencing tool at once.

Use Cases

Internal Communications – There is no better way to have a meeting than via a web conferencing tool; the keys are the ability to see and hear all the participants, screen sharing, and text chatting. It allows a geographically dispersed group the ability to feel closer and go over important matters, share information, or just have a team meeting or daily or weekly update. It is what the conference call used to be. During COVID-19 the use of web conferences went from something a lot of organizations used to one that now virtually everyone uses. Zoom changed how the world looked at web conferencing; they made it easy to use and very accessible for anyone. We have all been invited to Zoom happy hours, birthdays, and workout classes. One of my favorite parts is that you can access Zoom from any device and that I get to see and hear whomever I am engaging with.

Sales – To me this is one of the best use cases. It gives you the ability to see and hear your customers and prospects and it's the ideal way to share your slides, your screen, and demo your products and solutions right from your computer. It also can be scheduled but does not have to be; in other words you can just send out your custom link and anyone globally can log instantly on, and in a matter of minutes.

DETERMINING THE RIGHT PROGRAM FOR YOU

So now the hard part: What is the right solution for me? The good news is you don't have to pick one solution and you can always change your solution based on your use case.

One of my goals in this book is to give you the tools you need to make the shift to virtual and hybrid events, but it's also to take away some of the fear you have in making this transition. Trust me, you will make a few mistakes along the way, but as long as you are creating content that is high quality and engaging, the rest will be easy. I have also said before, one of the best parts of virtual events is no one has created the perfect mousetrap yet. I have produced and been part of thousands of events; I have made more mistakes and miscalculations than I can even remember, and I have helped create some of the best innovations and worked on some of coolest and most engaging events as well. So, for all we know it's going to be one of you reading this book who creates the next great virtual event innovation.

Take a deep breath and ask yourself these questions. After you've answered them, all the support information on what you should do next you'll find in chapters throughout the book.

- **What are your goals of the program?**
    - It could be attendance size
    - It could be number of engagements
    - It could be the time an attendee spends inside the virtual event
    - It could be the number of sessions or programs that the attendee watches
    - It could be the number of booths each attendee visits
    - It could be the number of qualified sales leads that you or your sponsors get
    - Is it brand recognition for your company or organization?
    - Is it about accreditations and learning?

- **What is the ROI (return on investment) you're looking for?**

  - Is it revenue from registrations?

  - Is it the revenue from exhibit booths sold?

  - Is it how many demonstrations your team can give during the days of the virtual event?

  - Is it the revenue from sponsorships?

  - Is it increasing membership?

  - Is it to increase your visibility?

  - Is it education related, in other words the number of certifications achieved?

  - Is it public relations related, the number of stories written about your events and sponsors?

- **How important is interaction?**

  - Is it the number of one-on-one interactions?

  - Do you want the audience to answer polls?

  - Do you want to test new products and offerings on your audience?

  - Do you want to have gamification and contests? (I will cover this in greater detail later in the book.)

  - Is it important for the attendees to interact with each other?

- **How important is video?**

  - Will your presentation be live video or prerecorded?

  - Will you enable your sponsors or exhibitors to add videos?

  - Will you create an event-opening video?

- Will you have your speakers present via their webcam, or will you send a video crew to their home or office, or will you have them go to a local studio, or will it be a combination?

- Will you want the ability to have multiple presenters from different locations on the screen at the same time?

- **How important is two-way video?**

  - For your breakout rooms

  - For your classroom programs

  - For media interviews

  - In your exhibitor's booth

  - Is it important to have the audience show their video when they ask questions during sessions?

- **How important is your support material?**

  - Slides

  - Product demos

  - Handouts for your presentations

  - Whitepapers

  - Screen sharing for breakout room presentations

- **What types of presentations will you have?**

  - General sessions

  - Keynote sessions

  - Breakout sessions

  - Training sessions

  - Fireside chats sessions

  - Will the presentation be live with question-and-answer periods?

- Will the presentation be simulated live with Q&A periods?

- Will the presentation be prerecorded or a combination of live, simulated live, and prerecorded?

- Will any of your presentations be audio and slides, or will it be video and slides, or will it be a combination of audio and video programs? (I am a big fan of video programs whenever possible. It not only gives your audience the ability to hear what the presenter is saying, it allows the audience to see the presenter's facial expressions and it makes it easier to engage with the presenter.)

- **How important is polling and/or surveying your audience?**

  - You have a unique opportunity to keep your audience involved in the program and not just voyeurs with polling and audience surveys.

  - Instant feedback may or may not be important to you, but it's something you need to plan for before the program begins.

- **Will you be having certifications or continuing education programs for credits?**

  - A lot of virtual events for associations, legal, healthcare, technology, and accounting organizations include the ability to earn continuing education credits. This could also be a good way to increase revenue as well.

  - You could also look into partnering with accreditation organizations.

- **Will you have multiple sessions at the same time?**

  - How many sessions will you want to be running at the same time?

  - One of the benefits of a virtual event or hybrid event is that the audience member can watch one session live and then go back and watch the other sessions at their leisure on-demand after the program is over. Remember you need to spend a lot of time planning and scheduling sessions, so make sure you don't take on too much for your first virtual event.

- If you have multiple sessions, make sure you make the agenda available before the virtual event begins and make sure you use a platform that allows the attendees to create their agenda in advance and save the session dates and times.

- **Where do you want your program to live after it is over?**

  - Will you keep the virtual event open? (Most platforms give you one year of access.)

  - Will you download your sessions and put them in your own content management system (CMS) or learning management system (LMS)?

  - Will you continue to add live and on-demand content to your virtual event platform after the program is over?

- **How important is the on-demand program?**

  - If you create good content, in my opinion you should repurpose it as much as you can. Your audience is not going to be able to watch and interact with everything during your virtual event.

  - On-demand is a great way to keep your virtual event populated after the live period is over.

  - You can also share some of the content after the program is over to your social media sites like Facebook, YouTube, Vimeo, Twitter, LinkedIn, or on your website.

- **How many days will your program last?**

  - A lot of organizations try to mirror what they have done in the past at physical conferences. In my opinion you're better off starting with a more manageable agenda until you master virtual event content creation. You have to have enough to fill the length of the program you decide on.

- Also don't forget about time zones. If it's a physical-only event, everyone is in the same time zone. But if it's virtual, you can have attendees from all over the world joining in many time zones, so you need to be clear so they can calculate when your event will start in their time zone.

- **Will you have a registration?**

  - Think about what information you want to gather and if you need to use some of that information to limit access to areas within the event based on what they paid or their job title (e.g. engineers will only have access to product development sections). Keep in mind the more registration fields that you add, the more people may be inclined to abandon before finishing their registration.

- **Will you be charging for your event?**

  - If you charge for the physical event, you should think about charging for access to your virtual event.

  - Many organizers offer tiered pricing and even offer a free version, which limits what the free attendee can see and have access to. If you're having a hybrid event, it is even more important to find that balance between what you should charge for your virtual event compared to what you are charging for your physical event.

- **Will you be syndicating you content?**

  - Will you be delivering your content to your social media locations, your website, or partner and sponsor sites? If yes, how much of the content will you syndicate?

  - Will you be creating an OTT channel (think Roku, Apple TV, and any Smart TV channel)? Many organizations social stream their general sessions to build excitement for the event and reach the media.

- **Will you have a moderator?**

  - A moderator is a host to lead your audience through the virtual event and agenda and keep you audience informed.

  - I believe a good professional moderator is a key component to any hybrid event and is the perfect addition to a virtual-only event as well. If you decide to have a moderator, I suggest you look for someone who has television news experience.

- **Do you want to have a news desk?**

  - A news desk can be set up at your physical event and your programming can be streamed to the virtual audience who can hear the news from the conference, and see interviews with attendees, sponsors, executives, and speakers.

- **How do you want your event to look?**

  - *Customizable Templates* – A virtual event allows you to add your event colors, logos, sponsor images, and some design elements, but for the most part you have a couple of standard templates to work with. Standard templates offer you the following advantages:

    - You're rushing to move your event to virtual because your event was canceled last minute. Standard event templates take less time to set up and can be launched in a shorter amount of time.

    - You have a very small team to help you with the design element and management of your program.

    - There is a cost savings and time savings. Since the virtual event provider does not have to build, design, or create anything from scratch, this will lower the professional service, project management, and design costs.

- *Custom Template Design* – If you have the time and want to make your event have the look and feel of your physical event or corporate campus, or you don't want it to look like other virtual events, you can have a designer create a custom template. If you take this route, be sure to follow these suggestions:

  - If your event is 8 to 12 weeks away, then you'll have time for custom creative.

  - You have a really good design team that you work with inside your organization or outside.

  - You have hired an experiential marketing firm and they have a design element they want to use.

Once you come up with the answers to the above questions, then you're ready to take the first step into the world of virtual events. The following chapter shows you how to make the move to virtual and hybrid events.

CHAPTER 3

Converting from Physical to Virtual

I f you need to convert a physical, in-person event into a virtual event, chances are something unexpected happened. Sadly, in 2020, in-person events began being canceled due to the pandemic caused by COVID-19. With federal and local governments mandating social distancing and the shutdown of businesses, corporations decided the risk was too high to host or send employees to a physical event or allow business travel of any kind.

Virtual events can reach people anywhere. All you need is an internet connection and you can immediately access educational and networking experiences with the same audience you were expecting at a physical event.

In this chapter, we'll look at the key elements of your physical event and I'll show you how you should start thinking about them differently as you convert to a virtual event.

COMMUNICATION IS KEY

If your physical event was canceled, moving to a virtual event impacts everyone involved. First and foremost, it means that people need to cancel flights, hotel reservations, car rental reservations, and more. Once you decide that your in-person event is going virtual, quickly move to communicate to all involved. Or if you just decided to move your traditionally physical event to a virtual one for the first time, it is imperative that you communicate with your audience.

Two key things to focus on are the "why" (e.g. clearly communicate why you made the decision) and the "what next" (e.g. provide any and all details you have about the virtual event).

The order in which you communicate is important. I recommend the following:

1. Event staff, both employees and third-party vendors

2. Sponsors: exhibitors for a trade show or executive sponsors for a corporate event

3. Speakers and presenters

4. Attendees

Create a customized email for each group and have it come from the person in charge of the event. Have the email sent from a "real" email address so that the person in charge can receive the replies.

Also, since emails can get stuck in spam filters or outright missed, divide up the contact lists and have your team reach out to people by phone.

Envisioning a New Virtual Reality

You know how you can take a Microsoft Word document and save it as a PDF? Such a seamless conversion does not exist with physical-to-virtual events.

Instead of playing the "conversion game" (e.g. I have 20 presentations at my physical event, so that means 20 webcasts in my virtual event), envision and design a compelling and unique virtual experience, using your physical event design as the foundation.

You don't need to migrate every element of your physical event into the virtual event. And don't forget that there are features and experiences available in a virtual experience that you can't provide at a physical event, the most important being data. Virtual events will give you a wealth of data about attendee engagement and their movements throughout the event.

Speaking of the foundation, here are the basic physical event elements your team can migrate to a virtual environment:

- Sessions (keynotes, breakout sessions, interviews, lectures, lightning talks, lunch talks, etc.) – these can be live or pre-recorded, run concurrently, or they can "follow the sun." Virtual sessions can be immediately turned to on-demand so if someone misses a session they can go back and watch the next day, week, or month.

- Networking events or networking areas – group and one-on-one chats as well as video chats are all available within a virtual space.

- Exhibitor booths – booths can be custom branded for each client, can feature product and demo videos, act as a repository for company assets, and enable group and one-on-one text and video chat.

- Lunch or coffee breaks — of course you can't serve food, but you can still schedule breaks during the day with fun content. One of my clients featured an alternate reality game (ARG). Teams of attendees competed against one another in an experience that mixed the virtual world and real world, in which story elements and outcomes developed in real-time.

- Physical signage – virtual events offer a wide arrange of options to place display and banner ads and other graphically unique ways to represent your brand and your sponsors.

- Post-event entertainment, such as concerts – think of ways you can engage attendees after the sessions conclude. How about a live performance that's streamed?

I have found the best virtual event experiences were those envisioned with a 100% digital mindset, shedding assumptions and expectations of what a physical event is.

REDUCING YOUR CARBON FOOTPRINT AND THE IMPACT ON THE ENVIRONMENT (ESG)

We've known for a long time that virtual events and webcasts are greener and more sustainable when it comes to connecting with audiences around the world. But now, we can actually prove and document their effectiveness and how they can impact your ESG strategy.

The definition of ESG (environmental, social, and governance) describes areas that characterize a sustainable, responsible, or ethical investment.

The *Financial Times Lexicon* defines ESG as "a generic term used in capital markets and used by investors to evaluate corporate behavior and to determine the future financial performance of companies." It is used by investors to evaluate corporations and determine the future financial performance of companies. It adds that ESG "are a subset of non-financial performance indicators which include sustainable, ethical and corporate governance issues such as managing a company's carbon footprint and ensuring there are systems in place to ensure accountability." They are factors in investment considerations, used in risk assessment strategies incorporated into both investment decisions and risk management processes.

How Is Carbon Savings Calculated?

While this is all very exciting, the big question is how is the savings calculated?

A panel within your webcast will allow you to display real-time carbon savings across an entire event, with individual attendees able to see their own contributions as well.

By using a simple equation, we can calculate each attendee's individual carbon savings and the event's savings.

When you first set up your event, you select a "location point," which is typically the city where the event would be held if attendees were visiting in person or the location of a company's headquarters.

Each attendee's "miles" are calculated based on their distance from that location, which is determined when attendees allow the platform to access their device's location.

Those miles are multiplied by 53.3 – the average amount of CO_2 generated per mile by an airplane. That number is then divided by 150 (the average number of passengers on a plane) to determine individual savings.

For example: If I were in New York attending a virtual event hosted in Chicago, my carbon savings would be a little over 280 lbs. New York is 788.9 miles from Chicago, so: $788.9 \times 53.3/150 = 280.32$.

This feature allows attendees to see firsthand how they are contributing to fewer CO_2 emissions, and it allows hosts to actively track and report on their environmental impact.

After the event concludes, you can download reports that allow you to view the event's carbon savings and each individual's savings.

CRAFTING YOUR DESIRED USER JOURNEY

While no two virtual event user journeys are the same, we recommend that you craft the desired user journey and optimize your strategy and plan around it. For example, do you want maximum attendance at your keynote presentation? Or, do you want to maximize visits to sponsor booths, so that exhibitors have the best lead generation results? Perhaps you want both. What order should they happen in: keynote attendance first, followed by booth visits? Or does the sequence not matter?

What time of the day will you start your event, and what time will you end each day of programing? Are you attracting a large international audience? What challenges will their local time zones create? Will you have to run some sessions a second or even third time? Will those sessions need to be prerecorded and run as a simulated live program?

Here are some ways you can guide attendees toward the desired user journeys.

Use the event schedule to drive actions

Users will consult the event schedule to decide what to do and when. Be intentional with the design of your schedule, keeping your desired user journey in mind. Don't schedule your two most sought-after speakers for the same timeslot, since half your audience will miss out. If you want to drive visits to sponsor booths, carve out times (e.g. 30 to 60 minutes or more) that are labeled as such. Use the virtual technology as an advantage; you can add reminder emails and inside the environment send updates to remind the audience where they should be next and update them throughout the journey.

Use design elements to guide users

The lobby is one of the most visited spaces in a virtual event. It's the place users land when they log in. Use key navigational elements in this area to guide users where you want them to go. This is the perfect area to have an opening video that also acts as an overview of the content and the virtual event space (where everything is and how to use it). As well it's a great area to have an information desk to help your attendees on their journey.

For example, if "attendee matchmaking" is a key business goal of your event, place a prominent call-to-action to that feature. Find strategic placements in other well-trafficked areas (e.g. the networking lounge) and provide a similar call-to-action.

Another example, if your goal is for your audience to visit as many of your exhibitor booths as possible, you highlight where the booths are located and even highlight key booths in the lobby.

Use platform features to get users where you want them

Let's face it: sometimes you need to escort a user to an area rather than subtly nudging them in the right direction. Use features like scheduled pop-up announcements to guide users to the next session or to a specific sponsor's booth.

Don't assume that attendees will follow the right path – sometimes they need to be told what to do.

Some of my favorite virtual events are the ones that not only allow me to map out my day and journey, but will also make suggestions, based on what I have already registered for. This is similar to the way Amazon figures out what I like based on my buying decisions and then makes suggestions for other purchases that I may also like. The system could recommend a session based on other sessions that I have registered to attend or let me know of a booth that has lot of information on that topic I am interested in. This is another reason that you should enable your attendees to rate sessions and make recommendations, because the best recommendations in my opinion are the ones that come from my peers.

REWORKING AND REASSIGNING

Converting a physical event to a virtual one will obviously require some reworking and reassigning. The depth and complexity of this step depends on timing. If your physical event was 12 months out and you moved it to a virtual event, fewer things need to be reworked. If your physical event was in one month and you moved it to a virtual event three months from now, there are a lot more moving parts.

While moving a physical event so close to its date is stressful, the good news is that you may be done collecting deliverables. In that case, it's mostly a matter of loading those deliverables into your virtual event platform.

Reworking dates, timelines, and deliverables

The first thing to rework are timelines and dates for key elements:

- Sponsor deliverables
  - Artwork and logos
  - Handouts to be available for download

- Video to be played at the booth
- Video to be available to watch
- Links to products and websites
- Giveaways
- Contact information
- Who will be managing the booth during exhibit hall hours?

- Speaker deliverables: whether your speakers will appear live or prerecorded will need to be decided as soon as possible. If you prerecord speaker sessions, you need to allocate about 30% more time than if all speakers were appearing live. You will need to gather:

  - Slide presentations
  - Handouts
  - Polling questions
  - Surveys
  - Photos of the presenters
  - Bios
  - Session overviews
  - Understand where they will be when they deliver their presentation, if it is live, and make sure you test in advance from that location using the computer and equipment they will use on the live day.
  - Make sure if it is prerecorded that the lighting and audio have been tested.

- Services from third-party suppliers:
  - Are they creating graphics?
  - Are they creating videos?

- Make sure they understand the timelines.
- Make sure they are given access to upload content.
- Make sure you train them on the virtual environment.
- Marketing and promotions:
  - Make sure you time your marketing in order to build the most excitement around the program.
  - Make sure that all your links work.
  - Keep your registrants engaged with the event and content by developing a nurturing campaign that starts at least four weeks out. Unlike a physical event, they won't be showing up at a conference center so it's important that they understand how to access the virtual event on the live day(s).
- Press interviews (if applicable) related to the event:
  - Make sure you set up a press schedule.
  - Make sure you use your social media to promote any significant press interviews.
  - Consider having press conferences streamed and promoted
  - Offer the media contact to your sponsors, exhibitors and key speakers.

Reassigning members of the event team

Once your updated timelines are complete, figure out how to reassign everyone on the physical event team:

- Work out cancellations with physical event suppliers (e.g. venue, food and beverage, audiovisual, drayage, registration staff).
- For third-party agencies, determine which ones provide services that are transferable (and relevant) to a virtual event.

- New roles for internal teams. While some decisions are easy (e.g. email marketing remains as email marketing), other roles may need an assignment from a physical task to a task in the virtual event environment.

PERFORMING DRY RUNS

Practice, Practice, Practice – there is no better format for this, and it is 100% needed, especially if this is your first time presenting at or managing a virtual event.

I recommend separate dry runs for speakers, exhibitors, and attendees.

For speakers, arrange for private sessions in which you train them on the online presentation platform. If slides will be used, load them in advance and show speakers how to advance them. If video will be used, show presenters how that works and how Q&A is handled.

Give the speaker tips on what to wear and on lighting; you can even give them tips on equipment they might want to purchase to enhance their presentation.

And finally, if this is their first time presenting online, get them used to "speaking into the abyss," where eye contact with attendees is not possible. Some people are great at presenting in a boardroom with a dozen or so people and some are great in front of hundreds or even thousands where you see the audience and hear their responses to your jokes, but learning to present to a virtual audience is a lot different and it is strange to not be able to hear and see those whom you are presenting to. So it's up to you to make sure you give these presenters all the tools they will need to feel comfortable in this new format.

For me personally, I love the energy I get from presenting to a live audience, but I find myself keeping to my script more. What I enjoy about performing for a virtual audience is that I find that I am more authentic and more in the moment. I feel like I am presenting only to one person and that one person is there to hear what I have to say. I also like the feeling of knowing that my audience can be anywhere in the world. The best part of presenting virtually for me is that I am only focused on my material and what I am saying, and I am not distracted by everything else that could be going on in the room. If you have any trouble with presenting virtually, just think of yourself on TV or having your own podcast and remember the audience wants to be there, because if they didn't, they are only one click away from leaving.

Presenter tip: I like to think about the power of one. What I mean by this is with every presentation you do, it's not about the size of the audience but the speaker's ability to inspire, educate, and motivate. In the world of business it only takes one person in the audience to want to buy your product or your company. Before you get ready to present, always think about the power of one – it makes a difference.

For exhibitors, provide windows of time during which they can log into the virtual event environment and get access to their virtual booth. Have them provide quality assurance (QA) on all their booth materials and test out features to ensure they fully understand how to utilize all the tools in their booth.

Use your internal team as a proxy for attendees and have them log into the environment pretending to be one and have some members of your team staff exhibitor booths.

Bottom line, get to know your platform. Just like you would walk the convention center floor and test all the equipment and inspect all the tradeshow booths, you have to do the same thing with your virtual environment; it is one of the keys to a successful event.

SAVE THE DAY

Moving a physical event to a virtual event is stressful – not only did something unexpected cause the move, but your team is usually in a time crunch to move the event to a digital format. The good news is that the virtual event platform gives you the ability to save the day, compared to an outright event cancellation. Remember to think outside the box and design an experience they'll all remember. When physical events become a reality again, all this work will still be relevant as you can integrate elements of your live event into virtual to create a hybrid event. I tell you more about that in the next chapter.

CHAPTER 4

Hybrid Events: The Best of Both Worlds

In the first few chapters I've touched on hybrid events and what they are, but let's dig in a little deeper here to really understand their value and why they should always be a part of your events strategy.

Hybrid events combine a physical event with a virtual component to create an integrated and interactive experience for all audience types. Hybrid events can extend your audience reach and generate new revenue opportunities for your business. In addition, the virtual components of a hybrid event enable you to supply content and entice a brand-new virtual audience who may decide to attend a future event in person.

Also, a hybrid event can take place in several physical locations connecting the virtual audience participating from anywhere in the world. I believe hybrid is going to be one of the growth areas in the space for the foreseeable future. In other words, instead of 1,000 people flying to one location and all sitting in one ballroom together, we have 100 people going to 10 different locations and being connected virtually while bringing in a 100% virtual audience as well. In my conversations with hotel chains and event planners, it is looking like this will be one of the ways organizations will be dealing with the new events reality.

In this chapter, I'll talk about the value of hybrid events, take you through the different hybrid event types I think are most successful, and then give you a step-by-step guide of how you can create that content.

ESTABLISHING YOUR HYBRID EVENT OBJECTIVES AND AUDIENCE

Strategy is critical to hybrid success; therefore, you must clearly define your objectives and metrics up front. When creating your strategy, answer these questions to help you discover the best way to lay out your hybrid event:

- Is your goal to cut costs?

  - Run more of your sessions virtually and run niche sessions or sessions for one large target audience as a physical event.

- Are you looking for a different channel to generate more revenue?

  - Taking your event hybrid now gives you sponsorship opportunities in the virtual platform that you didn't have before.

- Are you trying to increase audience size?

  - Focus the marketing of the virtual event on those who never attend your physical event, industries that you know may have travel restrictions, or new audiences that you may not have considered before, like students or academics, if applicable.

- Is increasing attendee engagement your main focus?

  - Look at creative ways that you can integrate your virtual and live audiences, like my Aerosmith example earlier in the book.

- Is it an insurance policy going forward?

  - You want to start getting your audience used to a virtual component just in case you need to take your event to 100% virtual again.

- Keep your program running after your physical event has concluded.

  - Increase attendee satisfaction by having content available for them to revisit after the event is over. If there are two sessions running at the same time that they really want to see, they don't have to choose if one of those sessions is available on-demand after the event ends.

Knowing your target audience will help you to decide what elements to incorporate into your hybrid event to make it more successful. Focus on your audiences' familiarity with technology and how comfortable they are using webcasting and online event software. You may decide to conduct prospect and customer surveys during the event planning process to help you create an event experience that is technologically appropriate and engages your audience.

After determining your target audience start thinking about what content you want included in the hybrid extension. Using a virtual platform allows you the flexibility to include the entire event program, a single day of programming, or only specific sessions. This allows you to craft the perfect virtual experience for the hybrid event. This is also the time when you can begin to think about the other elements of the hybrid extension like who will be included in the virtual exhibit hall and if you will include interactive games with contests and prizes, networking lounges, or a resource center.

CREATING AN INTEGRATED EVENT EXPERIENCE

When hosting a hybrid event it's important not to market the physical and virtual event separately; rather promote them as a single entity because that's what they are. I've seen clients try to segment their audience by those whom they want to come to the physical event and those they want to come to the virtual because they are afraid of cannibalization. This is the same event, just with one component that is physical and another that is virtual. By integrating the content and experience seamlessly, both audiences will experience the same event, messaging, and branding. You may even have attendees try out the physical event one day and attend virtually the next based on their availability and location or the location of the physical event.

As I said early on, cannibalization is a myth and trying to segment your audiences by the action you assume they will take will result in marketplace confusion and damage to your brand.

Let me tell you about another example that demonstrates why cannibalization doesn't exist. There was a time when NFL football games were not broadcast in the cities where the team played unless the game was sold out. They'd simply black out those games. The thought process was that if we made the game available on TV, then no one would go to the games at the stadium. There was nothing further from the truth and in fact it damaged their brand with fans who had no way to support their teams on game day due to a variety of factors that prevented them from going to the stadium. Once the NFL started to allow games to be televised, even if the game was not sold out, the NFL grew incredibly and the teams started to make more money because of the additional advertising and merchandising revenue. Fans saw how great the in-person experience was and it motivated them even more to do what they could to make it to games when they could, and the rest, as they say, is history.

CAPTURING HYBRID EVENT CONTENT

When developing hybrid event content, you'll be capturing and broadcasting content from the physical event location to your virtual audience. Following are some types of content you can capture.

Roving Reporter Interviews

The roving reporter enables you to take the virtual audience on a journey around the event space by conducting interviews with attendees, sponsors, and presenters directly from the show floor.

Typically, the roving reporter offers two styles of videos:

Attendee Vignettes

- Allow attendees the opportunity to share their ideas and insights
- Short (under three minutes each) videos highlighting an attendee's experience
- Attendees are asked questions by an on- or off-camera reporter
- Interview questions can appear on screen, via text

Sponsor Spotlights

- Allow sponsors to get the exposure that they are looking for
- Short (under three minutes each) interviews from sponsor booths
- Sponsor branding (logo on screen)
- Inclusion of B-roll/existing video assets
- Text and graphic overlays
- Can also provide HD video file to sponsor for distribution/ further monetization
- All session videos can start and or end with a short video from the sponsors

Testimonials

Customer testimonials are company or product endorsements or recommendations from your strongest customer allies that affirm the value of a product or service. Testimonials should be given by happy customers, voluntarily or upon a company's request. I always like to present this to a customer as a thank-you and an honor; it is human nature to want to help those who have helped you. It also gives them the spotlight and makes them opinion leaders in the space.

News Desk/Talk Show Interviews

You will need a centralized place that is the "home base" of your hybrid program. I recommend that you have a news desk or "talk show" set where your main anchors broadcast from and where they can bring in outside interviews and content throughout the show. News desk interviews can be broadcast live or can be prerecorded and broadcast as live.

"Broadcast as live" is sometimes a confusing term, either something is live or not, well not always. The example I like to use is your network news. If you watch the 5 o'clock news and the 6 o'clock news back to back, sometimes you'll notice the same story run during both live programs. How can the reporter do the same exact interview twice?

Let's use this example: on the 5 o'clock news we have live news anchors at the news desk who transition to a reporter in the field who interviews a witness to a car crash and that interview is also live. On the 6 o'clock news we still have our live news anchors but when they transition to that interview of the car crash witness, it's recorded but running during a live news program so it's "running as live."

Sponsor Demos

You can integrate sponsor content into your live programming. This is usually in the form of product demos in their booth or in a branded area they've secured like a conference room. These demos can be broadcast live during your program or prerecorded and run as live.

Sample Hybrid Event Workflow

I had a healthcare client that we worked with for a number of years whom we helped put together a robust, multi-day hybrid program. These are the workflows I developed for them to ensure that they captured quality content for each of the content types I just discussed.

Prerecorded Content: Roving Reporter

A single interviewer and camera person will interview attendees, speakers, or others at the physical event and content can be broadcast at the physical event and virtually.

- **Staff needed:** Roving crew, content producer, and roving reporter

- **Process:**

  - Roving crew would be deployed (camera mounted on tripod stand, with single light). A content producer would have approval on shot setup (what you see through the camera) and interview questions.

  - Once content is captured, the content producer would provide a video editor with guidance on how the interview should be edited (e.g. taking out pauses, or if the interview was interrupted) and give final signoff on the edits.

  - A video deliverable would be ready to appear on the program the following day.

- **Editing Guidelines:**

  - Lower Thirds Graphics: A lower third is a combination of text and graphical elements placed in the lower area of the screen to give the audience more information on who the speaker is.

  - Guest lower thirds include first/last name, title, and organization.

  - Interview questions prompted off-screen will be shown as text, full screen.

    - White background with black text, question written out

    - Your company's logo appears in lower right-hand corner of screen

- **General Guidelines:**

  - Have speaker confirm on camera their name and spelling, company name, and title.

  - Instruct speaker to look at the camera or toward off-camera interviewer when answering questions.

- **Shot Recommendations:**
- Vary shots between questions:
  - Start with a mid-shot, waist up and with any signage in the camera frame as necessary.
  - Switch to closeups at least every other interview.
  - You can also shift the interviewee's position in the camera frame.
    - If you need to shift during an answer, try to make movement as smooth as possible or pause interviewee and restart the answer once shifted.
    - *Be mindful* of signage in the background that is either of a competitor or not pertinent to the interview.
      - If interviewee mentions any specific booths nearby, get wide shots and signage shots after the interview.
- **Editing Notes:**
  - All of the prerecorded interviews need to be ready to go by the following day (things shot Thursday need to be edited and ready for Friday's show, for example).
  - Leave lower thirds up for five seconds when the guest first appears on camera.
  - Final edited video will start/end with bumper and musical bed.
  - To use in live feed, three seconds of pad (logo) will need to be added to the end of edited piece.

Prerecorded and Live Content: News Desk

These interviews would be captured in a news desk setting and run live during the event.

- **Staff needed:** Camera crew, content producer, and show host

- **Process**:
  - Interview questions would be created by content producer, approved by those you designate.
  - Once content is captured, content producer would provide video editor with guidance and give final signoff on edit.
  - Video deliverable would be ready to appear on the live program the following day.

- **Editing Guidelines:**
  - Graphics:
    - Guest lower thirds with first/last name, title, and organization.
    - If sponsored, sponsor logo appears in lower left-hand corner of screen or your company's logo appears in lower right-hand corner of screen.
  - General Guidelines:
    - Leave lower thirds up for five seconds when the guest first appears on camera.
  - Editing Notes:
    - All of the prerecorded interviews need to be ready to go by the following day (things shot Thursday need to be edited and ready for Friday's show, for example).
    - After each live block of continuous programming that runs, footage will need to be cut into individual interview segments (twice daily).
      - Final edited videos will start/end with branded graphic and branded audio.
    - **Prerecorded Interviews:** To use in live program, in the first three seconds a company logo will need to be added to the end of the edited piece, so your crew has time to switch from the prerecorded to the live program.

Live/Prerecorded Booth Interviews

In this example you would be interviewing sponsors or exhibitors in their booth.

- **Staff needed:** Camera crew, content producer, and show host
- **Process:**
  - Interview questions would be created by content producer and approved by client.
  - After each hour of live broadcast, footage needs to be downloaded onto external hard drive and given to editors to cut into individual interview clips.
  - Each afternoon, editors need to cut entire morning's program into individual interview clips and deliver to content producers. These clips will be available to replay during live programming.
  - Content producer will confirm that each day's full show has been transferred to their hard drive.
- Sponsorship Content Editing Guidelines:
  - Graphics:
    - Guest lower thirds with first/last name, title, and organization.
    - If sponsored, sponsor logo appears in lower left-hand corner of screen or company appears in lower right-hand corner of screen.
  - General Guidelines:
    - Have the speaker confirm on camera their name and spelling, company name, and title (ideally in a full sentence).
    - Make sure to frame speaker in his or her booth surrounded by their organization's branding.

- Instruct speaker to look at host when answering questions.

- Make sure speaker does not stand in one spot for the entire interview. Have them show us around their space.

- If they are doing a product demo, speaker needs to make sure to pay full attention to the demo while talking through everything he or she is doing.

- Shot Recommendations for Demonstration:

  - Focus on getting a mid-shot (waist up) at the beginning of the demo.

  - Capture wide shots of booth.

  - Closeups of main things on display.
    - When possible, if any parts of the process are running long, move the camera with the demo, try to get closeups of what is being done.

    - Get closeups of any instruments/tools being used.

  - If another person is performing/explaining the activity, get shots of them repeating any pertinent information.

  - *Be mindful* of signage in the background that is either of a competitor or not pertinent to the interview.

- Editing Notes:

  - All of the prerecorded interviews need to be ready to go by the following day (things shot Thursday need to be edited and ready for Friday's show, etc.).

  - Leave lower thirds up for five seconds when the guest first appears on camera.

  - Final edited video will start/end with bumper and musical bed.

  - To use in live feed, three seconds of pad (logo) will need to be added to end of edited piece.

ACHIEVING BUSINESS GOALS BEYOND THE LIVE PERIOD

The main difference between a physical and virtual event is that once the live days are over, the event has concluded but a virtual event can still live on. Virtual attendees will have access to on-demand sessions, sponsor content, and online documents that they may not have had time to access during the live days of the virtual event. This allows for continued engagement in the event and with the sponsors or presenters.

One of the best parts of the virtual event is that once the days of the program are over, it is an opportunity to amplify your content. You can now use the content to continue the dialogue with your attendees and even attract new attendees to your organization and company by marketing the on-demand period of the event.

TAKING ADVANTAGE OF ATTENDEE FEEDBACK

Virtual events give you an incredible insight into the minds and actions of your attendees. Take advantage of it and leverage that power to deliver better online and hybrid experiences.

Direct Event Feedback

You will be able to find out which online participants logged in and out of your session or spaces, who clicked on links you shared, downloaded attachments, participated in chats, earned badges, or filled out surveys and polls. Using the robust drill-down information from each of these data points will help you to understand your audience and measure the success of the event, sponsor, or individual session. With a physical event that has no virtual component, it is incredibly hard to gauge audience involvement and measure the effectiveness of your techniques.

Indirect Feedback

Use social listening and media monitoring tools to understand what attendees are saying about your event and your organization on social channels like Facebook, Instagram, and Twitter, for example. PR reporting tools will give you access to what attendees are saying in print, on television, on podcasts, and will even report on blogger content. This data is very crucial, and I believe every event organization needs to pay attention to what the world is saying.

As you can probably tell after reading this chapter, hybrid is one of my favorite ways of delivering content and engaging with the audience. I really love the ability to take the best of both worlds and mash them together! I think the trend we will see for the next couple of years is not only the larger physical events transitioning to the world of hybrid, but the use of hybrid events will drastically change. More and more events will be executed on a smaller scale, happening simultaneously in various cities around the country or world, with let's say 100 or fewer people at each location, and content will be delivered to each of those locations from the other locations and from virtual presenters as well. The audience physically in a room will have two-way content beamed into that room from another location, so the hybrid virtual audience will not only be the remote audience participating at home or the office, but can interact with the physical audience as well, and that opens up an entirely new and unique way to engage with all of your audiences at once. Having the ability for these remote audiences to still have the physical networking and engagement opportunities to conduct business is a game changer.

CHAPTER 5

Virtual Event Planning 101

It goes without saying that in today's world, a virtual event planner has never been more important. To be successful you'll need to think about how to deliver your event differently, but many of the skills you've already mastered easily translate to the virtual event world.

In this chapter, I'll talk about the different elements that can make your event unique, setting your event strategy and goals, the importance of an engagement strategy and the engagement tools that virtual events can offer you.

YOUR ENTRYWAY TO VIRTUAL EVENT PLANNING

If you're not doing virtual event planning today, you're likely in one of two scenarios:

- You're a digital marketer (e.g. branding, demand generation, social media marketing), who's been given the task of planning and executing virtual events.

- You're an event planner (e.g. face-to-face events and meetings) who's adding virtual event planning responsibilities to your job description.

Given the current response to the COVID-19, you might be "thrown into the fire" and asked to plan a virtual event right away, with no formal training or knowledge of virtual events.

Note: For those who have time to plan, do online research about virtual event planning and consider going for an industry certification. One of the best-known industry certifications for virtual events is the Digital Event Strategist (DES) Certification from the Professional Convention and Management Association (PCMA) with over 7,000 members in 37 countries around the world. PCMA notes that there are 400+ DES graduates from 19 countries. This is a small number compared to the 12,000+ meeting professionals who hold the Certified Meeting Professional (CMP) certification. This means that a DES certification helps you stand out from the crowd, putting you among a relatively exclusive group of meeting pros.

I do believe that you will start to see courses, degrees, and even masters programs offered by colleges and universities around the world in a short time, or even by the time you're reading this book.

VIRTUAL EVENT PLANNING TIPS

While there are aspects of face-to-face events that can't be reproduced online, virtual events have attributes that are exclusive to the online experience. Virtual events can foster more open and direct communication. In a virtual "town hall meeting," for instance, employees may feel more comfortable sharing concerns about the workplace than if they were standing in an auditorium in front of all their co-workers.

Let's consider some tips for virtual event planners.

Identify Your Target Audience

Just like with your physical event, it's important to clearly document your target audience personas and plan for their needs in your virtual event. Now that your event is virtual, you can market to a wider audience than before because travel and time out of the office is not an issue.

What type of audience are you looking to attract that you thought might never come to your physical event because of travel or cost restrictions? Your virtual target audience shouldn't be exactly the same as your physical target audience – think bigger, think global!

Think Beyond the Livestream

Yes, the livestream is a primary element of the event experience. In a virtual event, the livestream covers the audio or video presentations (e.g. keynotes, main sessions, breakout sessions) – in short, all your content.

Don't get me wrong: spend the time, money, and effort to deliver a high-quality livestream. But also think deeper about how you can meet the needs of your online audience. Understanding what types of content appeal to the various segments of your participants in a virtual environment is essential. If you simply stream content from a stage, the online audience will not feel included. You need to take advantage of the engagement tools a virtual environment provides, like real-time Q&A, polling, and live chat.

If you understand what your online audience wants and create an experience to meet those needs, you'll stand out from other event planners. Not many digital event producers understand the education and engagement piece, so if you can master that strategy, you've developed a useful skill that will set you apart from people who only know how to broadcast content.

Craft a Unique and Compelling Virtual Experience

It's a common mistake: experienced event pros planning their first virtual event seek to replicate face-to-face experiences online. The problem? Not everything in a face-to-face event translates well to an online experience. In addition, by focusing solely on replicating a face-to-face event experience, you miss out on exclusive opportunities that an online experience provides.

Don't assume that a great digital event is the same as a successful live event. It requires a lens that is clearly focused on an audience you cannot see and who may or may not stay engaged depending on the production and true value of the content being delivered.

While virtual event planners will have less ability to gauge body language and facial expressions, proxies can be used to measure engagement, like the number of questions asked during a webcast, the number of users in a networking lounge, number of one-on-one chat messages exchanged, etc.

In addition, ensure that your engagement strategy makes use of the features provided by the virtual event platform. You don't know what attendees are really paying attention to because they're not with you, so you need to have a really engaging strategy to combat the attention deficit that will be in play.

Engagement Features

Mention the term "user-generated content" and most people think of blogs (e.g. Medium, WordPress) or forum sites like Reddit and Quora. On these sites, users publish questions, opinions, and perspectives and invite others to weigh in.

In a virtual event, user-generated content is how attendees engage with each other, and if a platform doesn't have these options, your event won't have as much value to attendees as a platform that does.

Here are a few examples:

Moderated chat

Think of an "Ask Me Anything" session that features your keynote speaker. A moderated chat session enables the speaker to engage with the audience via text-based chat. Audience members submit questions and comments. On the back end, a moderator views comments and questions and decides whether to approve or reject each one. The speaker can then post responses and comments publicly or privately.

Networking lounge

The networking lounge is an open and unmoderated group chat area where attendees can gather, meet, and converse. Think of it like a "group text," in which people post comments and others reply. Attendees like to visit the networking lounge to see who else is attending the event and to ask each other about favorite sessions.

Private chat

In addition to the open, public chat supported in the networking lounge, attendees can initiate private, one-on-one chat with other attendees. Think of it like the conversation that's sparked when standing in the food line at a physical conference. In addition, when visiting a sponsor's virtual booth, attendees can initiate private chat sessions with booth representatives who are online at the time.

All of the above examples could also be video chats, where both the attendees' and moderators' video and audio are also transmitted. So as you're thinking about your engagements make sure you understand your audience, and remember you don't have to do all of your engagements the same way; mix it up a little.

Gamification

Gamification is the use of game design techniques, including game mechanics and game dynamics, to drive participation, engagement, and loyalty with an audience. To understand game mechanics is to understand human desires and motivations.

In all walks of life, we strive for reward, status, achievement, self-expression, competition, and altruism. Game mechanics can be used in virtual event platforms to drive engagement around these desires. Game mechanics include points, levels, challenges, virtual goods, leader boards, gifting, and charity.

Gamification can be used to achieve the following results in a virtual event:

- Drive traffic to sponsor booths

- Increase audiences for sessions

- Improve peer-to-peer networking

- Increase content consumption from attendees

- Build audience loyalty

- Encourage audience members to join social media conversations about the event

- Increase participation in polling and Q&A during webinar sessions

Before you deploy these tactics, you need to consider the following:

- Understand what constitutes a "win" for your event

- Design for the emotional human, not the rational human

- Provide meaningful intrinsic and extrinsic rewards

- Interactions can sometimes be boring: make everything a little more fun

Gamification will be a powerful tool for you to drive attendee engagement and will also provide you with options to include in sponsorship packages. I'll go into more detail on this in Chapter 7.

ESTABLISHING YOUR EVENT STRATEGY AND GOALS

Before getting into the nuts-and-bolts of virtual event planning, it's important for your entire team to agree on the event's strategy and goals.

It may seem counterintuitive, but when planning a virtual event, it's important to think about the end of your event first. When the "lights" go out and everyone leaves, what is it that you hope to have accomplished? Do you want to be seen as the dominant thought leader? Are you looking to attract thousands of new top-of-the-funnel leads? Will you be measured on how many people purchase a product or service from you in the next three to six months? Are you trying to motivate, engage, and reward your employees or customers? All of these questions and more should be answered before identifying what type of virtual event you should run. Knowing the end result, identifying the metrics you want to achieve, and then working backwards will lead to the most successful virtual events.

Once you have identified the end results, you can start thinking about the length of your virtual event (both the live period and the on-demand period), the agenda of your event, what type of content will help drive your end results, whom will you invite to your event, and what type of engagement with your audience you are after. All of these individual pieces must be looked at concurrently as they each impact the others. For example, an event with 50,000 people is going to demand different types of engagement than say an event with 300 people. An event with 50,000 people will also have an impact on the type of content you need to produce.

A lot of people we talk to believe that a virtual event can't be two, three, or four days in length, but that isn't true. A successful multi-day event is absolutely possible if you plan for the event with the attendee's journey in mind. Only after the strategy of the event is set should you start worrying about features and functionality. If done correctly, this part will actually be the easiest because you can now map the platform's available functionality to the business outcomes you are trying to achieve. A perfect example of this is the exhibitor experience.

If you have an exhibit hall, and one of the goals of the event is to drive engagement at the booth level, employing gamification through a badging program can drive the audience to have the interactions the host desires. Instead of just announcing that the exhibit hall is open and staffed, reward people with a badge for visiting at least 10 of the booths, or you can even go one step further and create two levels of badges, one for visiting 50% of the booths, and one for visiting all of the booths. Going back to the beginning, if your goal as the organizer of the show was to drive thousands of people to your exhibitors' booths for meaningful interactions, you will have now achieved this feat and can call this part of your event a success.

Establish and Document Business Goals

Determine what your key goals are and how a virtual event can help you to achieve them. The goals below are some common ones for my clients, and I explain how a virtual event can address these differently than a physical event.

Generate Sales Leads

If your goal is to increase leads, a virtual event is an incredible way to generate sales leads for a marketing event or for an event that is going to have exhibitors or sponsors. At a physical event your attendee has to seek you out or set up meetings before the event happens so that you can coordinate a place and time. Once you're onsite you can only collect leads when someone hands you a business card or if you scan their conference badge; during a virtual event we are tracking every movement of each attendee. We know who came to your booth, we know what whitepapers or documents they have downloaded, and we know if they chatted with one of your booth attendees or one of your sales reps. Based on all these actions, you can develop a lead scoring model and provide your salespeople with important information about each lead.

Move Existing Prospects Further Down the Sales Cycle

The first thing that a prospect will do is register for your event by filling out a registration form. You can build your form to capture prequalifications so you will know what your attendees' main goals are and you can customize their experience in order for them to get the most out of your event. You can then deliver your attendees with targeted content in breakout sessions, one-on-one video chats, live Q&A sessions with your product experts, hands-on learning labs, and live and on-demand demos.

Educate Resellers and Partners on Your Latest Products

This is a really good use of the virtual event format because you can train your partners and resellers on your products and solutions and while they are inside the event they can take quizzes and exams and participate in hands-on labs in order to get their certifications.

The pharmaceutical, accounting, technology, and legal community has been enabling online, virtual continuing education and certification for years by using virtual events.

Educate, Reward, and Recognize Your Sales Team

Yearly sales kickoffs are one of my favorite use cases for a virtual event. We've done our sales kickoffs as hybrid events and also 100% virtual. At first you think that you can't get the same interaction and engagement as you can with a face-to-face sales meeting, I think the only thing you lose is the ability to actually see your colleagues in person, but you gain so much more. Your sales event can still offer training, business updates, one-on-one demos, and role playing. Offer regional breakouts, opportunities for recognition, and gamification to keep your attendees engaged. I also believe you need to theme your sales kickoff. My company's sales kickoff in 2020 had a decades theme. All my executives and I were given a decade and we had to dress as our favorite celebrity of that decade. My decade was the 1980s and I did my keynote dressed like Axl Rose of Guns N' Roses. It was fun and it lightened the mood while also helping to immediately engage my audience and set the tone for the two-day event.

EVALUATING PLATFORM OPTIONS

This is an important decision on your road to having a successful event; your virtual event is an extension of your organization's brand!

When I first got involved in virtual events, I viewed the virtual environment as the movie theater and the movie was the content in general sessions and breakout sessions. It was for that reason that in 2010 I wanted to acquire a virtual event company. I had already been in the streaming and hybrid space for over 10 years and knew that even though the audience comes for the content it needed to live in an interactive environment, where you can

(continued)

(continued)

connect with sponsors and customers and get various kinds of content while delivering incredible analytics and reporting. That is when I truly realized the power of the virtual event and it led me to the acquisition of Unisfair in 2010 and then in 2018 the acquisition of INXPO, which is the largest virtual event platform on the market and has a leading webcasting/steaming platform called Studio.

The good news: there's a wealth of options for you to choose from. The options range from webinar and web meeting platforms on one end to three-dimensional, immersive experiences on the other end.

Capture that vision in a one- or two-page document, then map your vision to a technology platform that best delivers on it. For example, if your vision is simply to host five live webinars with audience Q&A, then look to the many webinar platforms that exist.

If, on the other hand, you have a more complex vision that includes live video, one-on-one and one-to-many audience interaction, immersive exhibitor booths, audience matchmaking, and other "fancy features," then look for a platform that can make these elements a reality.

When engaging with a vendor's sales team, share the one- or two-page vision document up front and ask that all sales demos demonstrate how their platform delivers on your vision. In addition, ask for references from other customers who ran an event like yours. Speak to those customers and, better yet, ask if the event can still be accessed.

Define Your Format, Style, and Personality

Consider the style and personality of your virtual event. Your technology platform will provide pre-existing event templates. You can choose from their library and apply a certain amount of customization. While this option is efficient for both time and cost, you may decide that you want a distinctive and 100% custom-developed design. It is really important that your virtual event fits into your brand. So, spend a lot of time on this with your creative team; remember, from the moment your attendees log into your event, it is a representation of your organization.

So, think about if you want a responsive-style event or a 2D or 3D style. Do you want it to be fun and bouncy or should it be more serious and technical?

A responsive or 2D design environment is based on a flat grid layout and uses simple buttons and labels, similar to a web page. This design option is a bit more content forward and can typically look like an extension of your company website.

A 3D environment uses angles, texture, and depth to give users the feeling that they're in a three-dimensional space. A 3D environment may also use visually rich photography to make users feel like they're walking through a convention center, an outdoor veranda, or an elaborate exhibit hall. This design option is focused more on the visual experience with the content integrated within it.

Most virtual event platforms provide "3D-like" experiences: The event areas render with the depth of 3D but aren't truly immersive. Users are not able to travel through an immersive experience like they would in the 3D virtual world of Second Life.

2D Features

- Content-focused experience via a website look and feel

- Full responsiveness on mobile (iOS/Android/Windows)

- Branding capabilities without space restriction

- Provides a look that is more familiar to users

3D Features

- Full-screen event experience

- Serves the desktop user with a more robust visual experience

- Mobile compatible (iOS/Android/Windows)
- Full branding capabilities (can include custom Photoshop and .PSD files)

Create a Written Business Plan That Details Measurable Business Goals

Share the plan with the entire team, solicit feedback, and get buy-in and approval from the executives who are funding the virtual event.

At the conclusion of the virtual event, you'll report on the measurable business goals to determine its overall success.

Now that you have your business objectives and fundamental strategy in place, you have to think about how you're going to execute. You can't do it without the amazing people on your team. In the next chapter, I'll talk about the key roles you'll need on your team to make your event a success.

CHAPTER 6

Assembling Your Virtual Event or Hybrid Event Team

Your virtual event is going to have as many elements and moving parts as a physical event. You still need to create content, book speakers, and sell booth spaces, as well as manage the build-out of the environment. In order to do all this successfully, you need a combination of marketing and event planning skills, technological expertise, and content development capabilities.

Allowing plenty of planning time will enable these teams to work together to make your event a success. As a side note, if you are running a hybrid event, you will need to have a physical event team *and* a virtual event team. Many times, I've seen companies try to have the same people do both and the results leave you with team members who are overwhelmed and who prioritize the physical event over the virtual. You cannot take a physical event and set up cameras in the back of the room and deliver the exact same content in the exact same format to your virtual audience as you would for your physical event, so it is very important that you put together the right team with business ROI for both the physical and virtual portions of the event.

I believe you will need a minimum of eight to ten weeks to plan a successful virtual event. If this is going to be a hybrid event, you should start promoting the virtual portion at the same time as you plan and promote the physical event, so keep that in mind when creating your planning team.

This chapter provides detailed guidance on assembling your dream team for a virtual event or a hybrid event. Remember, this is your event and you need to make sure that everyone on the team is on the same page and has the same vision and mission as you do. So, let's get started.

VIRTUAL EVENTS

Most of your physical event team can transition easily to take on the responsibilities of virtual events. You'll have exhibitors and sponsors to manage but now you'll be more hands-on as they build out their own virtual spaces. There is an abundance of sponsorship opportunities in a virtual event so you'll need to build new packages from scratch, but don't worry, I have a chapter on that. There will still be speakers to manage but you'll just need to get them used to presenting on camera. My point is that you have the skill sets already on your team; they will all just need to learn some new skills and think like an online viewer.

When you begin to staff for hybrid events, you need to start to learn as much as you can about TV and video production because that's the staff members you'll need to have on your team or hire.

Depending on the size of your event, these roles will have teams supporting them, but these are the key team members you will need to have on your team.

Event Lead

This is the owner of the event who makes all strategic decisions and is ultimately responsible for the success of the event. The event lead will choose all the team members and assign roles, be the owner of the budget, determine event dates, select vendors, and report progress up through his or her leadership team.

This person will also make the final decisions on the "site map" of the event: for example, how many theatres (location to watch and interact with content) will be included, will there be gamification, how will the environment be customized, etc.

The event lead should be present at all vendor meetings and leading internal meetings. The event lead is also the point of escalation for the internal team and for all vendors. A good way to look at the event lead is if he or she were your general contractor if you were building a house.

Sponsorship Development and Management Lead

This is the individual who works directly with exhibitors and event sponsors. He or she is responsible for selling the benefits of sponsor and exhibitor participation. In addition, this team member will develop all of the sponsorship packages, market these opportunities to potential sponsors, and train the internal sales team on how to sell exhibit spaces and sponsorships.

By the time these activities are taking place, you've already selected your virtual platform. I would recommend putting together one or two exhibitor and sponsor webcasts that can be 30 to 45 minutes with 15 minutes for Q&A. This is a great way to introduce your sponsors and exhibitors to the benefits of virtual, walk them through all exhibitor and sponsorship options available, and answer all initial questions at the beginning of the sales cycle. You should also make these videos available for on-demand viewing as well, and if your exhibitors and sponsors are global, you need to deliver these events in various time periods so that they have the ability to engage and ask questions as well. I believe it is important to also engage with this audience on a regular cadence before the event.

In addition, this person will need to determine how sponsorship fulfillment is handled:

- *Pre-event Fulfillment* – Coordinating with sponsors and exhibitors to collect all content and creative assets within the timelines set for them and ensuring that all assets are laid out in the environment per the agreement. Each sponsor and exhibitor should have a clear point of contact in the pre-event phase where questions can be directed.

- *Pre-event Fulfillment (Speaker Sponsorship)* – If you have sold speaking sponsorships, you will have to work closely with your content management lead to get your sponsor on the agenda and ensure that all elements of the presentation that were sold are executed as part of the agenda.

- *Post-event Fulfillment* – Ensure that sponsors and exhibitors receive all event data that was promised to them per their agreement; create a post-event report for each sponsor and exhibitor and conduct debrief calls with all of them. During the debrief calls, your sales team should be discussing opportunities for the next year's event and reminding larger sponsors about first-right-of-refusal deadlines for the following year.

Content Management Lead

This is the person or team who develops the content strategy, including themes and messaging, builds out the agenda, and recruits and manages speakers.

In this role, this person will need to determine how the schedule will be laid out and make the following determinations:

- How many days should the event run?

- What time will the event begin and end each day?

- How many hours of content will be broadcast each day and how many exhibit hall breaks will you want?

- Does any aspect of the agenda need to be multilingual and how will translations be handled?

- If this is a global event, will the agenda "follow the sun"? When the agenda follows the sun, that means that the agenda is broadcast as live to all regions (APAC, EMEA, North America, etc.).

- Will you have tracks and, if so, how will those content tracks be organized? Most often tracks are organized by topic or area of expertise, etc.

- What will be the format for each session (single speaker, panel, etc.)?

- Do you have sessions that are eligible for certification or educational credit? If you do, you will need to coordinate with the accreditation institutes and your vendor to determine what actions will fulfill the certification or educational requirements. Virtual event platforms can push out exams at the end of a session, conduct polls during sessions, and measure the time a person stays in a session.

- Will the entire event be broadcast live, a combination of live and prerecorded sessions, or will all sessions be prerecorded?

- How will Q&A be handled? Will it all be live or text-based Q&A?

In addition to figuring out the agenda structure, the content management lead will need to manage all the speakers. If you have over 10 to 12 speakers, I would recommend that you assign one or more people to manage those speakers. A rule I like to use is to assign one person per 12 to 15 speakers if the speaker coordinator is not 100% dedicated to the event. If the speaker manager is completely dedicated to the event, this number can be 30 or 40.

Marketing and Promotions Lead

The individual is responsible for developing a marketing strategy and messaging to drive awareness and registrations of the virtual event. This person will also be responsible for your lead management strategy and reviewing and reporting on the event data.

These are the main areas of focus for your marketing team member:

- *Outline Marketing Goals* – Strategize on how you will achieve your objectives to make selecting the right channels easier. Also don't just think about online promotions; the event might be virtual, but your promotion does not have to be 100% virtual as well.

- *Segment Your Audience* – Personalize your message by what is important to each group.

- *Develop Your Messaging* – Remember, messaging should be slightly different for each channel. If virtual is new to your audience, emphasize how they can network, engage with speakers, and how easy it is to navigate the environment. They'll need reassurance that attending will be easy and that they will get to interact with others and not just watch a bunch of videos.

- *Multiple Marketing Strategies* – Make sure to have a strategy in place for pre-event, during-the-event, and post-event marketing and select which marketing channels you will use for each strategy.
  Think about where and when you want to syndicate your program to reach your intended audience.

- *Build the Calendar* – Schedule your promotions to balance the reach of all your channels so you are not relying too heavily on one channel over the other.

- *Define a Lead Scoring and Distribution Model* – Familiarize yourself with the available data your platform provides to build out your model.

- *Define Metrics* – Discuss how you will measure success to stay on track to meet your goals.

In addition to external marketing channels, this person will also manage the development and messaging of the registration and log-in pages, any attendee emails that are generated from the virtual event platform, as well as messaging for any other available features (pop-up ads, marquee messaging, etc.).

Event Planner

I know a lot of event planners are nervous about the shift to virtual and if there will be a need for their services. I truly believe the planner is almost needed more for a successful virtual event than a physical event.

This is going to be a huge growth area, and all event planners going forward will need knowledge and experience in producing virtual events. University and event associations are scrambling to develop and offer classes on how to create and produce virtual events. This is rapidly becoming a must-have on your resume.

I recently had a conversation with one of the largest experiential event companies, and their CEO is in the process of cross-training all of their producers, planners, and designers on how to create and manage virtual events. This CEO 100% believes that the future is hybrid and virtual and that his team has to be even more creative to keep the attention of a virtual attendee.

The event planner wears many hats and the person in this role will be the liaison between his or her team and the virtual event vendor's project manager to ensure that his or her team is meeting all the deadlines to get the event built.

Here are just a few of the things that he or she will be responsible for:

- Collection of all assets that need to be included in the virtual event
- Keeping all spreadsheets and other tracking tools up to date for the team

- Ensuring that the virtual event project manager is informed of any updates or changes that the event planner's team has made

- First one to review and provide feedback on any parts of the event before those elements go out to the wider team

Hybrid Events

In addition to the roles above, if you are creating a hybrid event, you will need a production team. Based on the length and complexity of your production, you may not need all these roles and sometimes one person can take on multiple roles. However, it's important to know what function each person will play to make your hybrid event successful.

Executive Producer/Show Runner

The executive producer leads the production team and holds ultimate management and creative authority for the program and will be the main program contact. This person will need to be 100% aligned with what your organization goals and ROI for this program are.

We have found that individuals with a broadcasting and event background are some of the best executive producers for a virtual event. That's because they are used to keeping to a tight timeline and are good at delegating and thinking on their feet. Plus, producing a broadcast for television is a lot like a virtual event.

On the show days, the executive producer is in charge of the flow of the entire production and should be the one who briefs each speaker to make sure they are comfortable and happy with how their segments/session will flow.

To me the most important element the executive producer brings to the show should be the ability to be ready for anything and make swift last-minute decisions. They must have a handle on the what-ifs:

- What happens if a presenter doesn't show up?

- What happens if a session runs too short?

- What if there is technical issue?

- What is the backup if anything goes wrong?

- What if the client or sponsor wants to make last-minute changes or is unhappy?

The executive producer has to deal with any and all crises, no matter how big or small.

Director

I think of the director as the person who is telling everyone what to do. He or she decides which camera or graphic/video will be shown at any given time, directs camera operators to adjust shots, gives feedback on composition, and keeps the broadcast on time. The director should be involved pre-show to coordinate and advise on how the program and format will work.

He or she has to know the program from start to finish and has to be prepped with all speaker support that every presenter will be using for their program. A good director will give the presenters feedback and pointers to make their presentation the best they can be for the show.

To me the most important thing a good director could do is rehearse the entire program, multiple times. There is no such thing as too much pre-program preparation.

Technical Director

The technical director is responsible for video switcher deployment and configuration. He or she listens to instruction from the director and makes them on the video switcher.

The technical director works with camera operators to execute the director's direction for camera and graphics coloring, shading, and general calibration. A good technical director is always thinking three or four moves ahead of the program.

Producer

The producer assists with interviewee scheduling and ensuring they arrive on time.

He or she works with the floor manager (see definition below) if adjustments need to be made on set on the fly. The bigger the program is, the more producers you'll need. You could have one producer just handling general sessions, one who handles breakout room productions, one who handles remote video and programs, and one who is responsible for all preproduced graphics and videos. They'll all work together to put all those pieces of your program puzzle in place.

Production Assistant

The production assistant performs various production-related tasks as needed and is vital to setup and testing of the overall production.

Graphics Operator

The graphics operator configures the equipment that provides video and graphics playback during the program. He or she takes cues from the director on when to start/stop visuals and when video playbacks are running.

Encoding Technician

The encoding technician is responsible for the configuration and monitoring of all live streaming equipment for every unique connection.

Floor Manager

The floor manager is the liaison between the production team and activities on the set. He or she gives time and schedule cues to the speakers and works with the director to ensure the show stays on schedule.

Editor

The editor manages all pre- and postproduction video editing needs during the event.

Camera Operator

The camera operator sets up and controls all camera operation and functionality and takes cues from the director to make adjustments as needed.

Audio Engineers

Audio engineers are responsible for quality audio mix for onsite audiences and makes adjustments to audio mix per interviewer and video playback(s).

He or she monitors microphone settings and controls the volume of each speaker and ensures that everyone is "mic'd" correctly and on time.

With your team now in place for a virtual or hybrid event, I'm dedicating the next chapter to walking you through detailed steps on how to adapt your content to virtual.

CHAPTER 7

Adapting Your Content for Virtual

J ust as with your physical event, your content is going to be the main factor that is driving attendance. As I mentioned earlier in this book, it's easy to play the "conversion game" and just drop physical event content into your virtual event, but the two environments are different.

Physical events have space limitations and time limitations that you don't have with virtual. You may only have rented a convention center for three days and you need to squeeze 100 sessions into those three days. In a virtual event you could run your event over five days or take all those sessions and run them over two separate events in order to better segment your audience. You could also take some of those sessions that traditionally have lower attendance and run those as individual webcasts.

Virtual events give you more flexibility and choices so you have to think strategically and not cut and paste from a physical environment to a virtual one.

In this chapter, we'll look at the best time to run your event, how to break out your programming in webcasts as well as throughout the environment, and how to make the event's engagement tools work for you.

BEST PRACTICES WHEN OUTLINING YOUR EVENT'S CONTENT

One of the first questions I usually get when clients are trying to lay out their content is on what days and times should I run my event to get the largest, most engaged audience. I see this more as a content than planning question because there's a strategy to the answer. You have to look at different factors directly related to your content to answer this question.

Is your industry seasonal in nature? For example, if you're running an event for accountants, then April 14 is not the right day to have it. If your event is for those in the hospitality industry, choosing a Friday or a Saturday won't be a good fit.

My general recommendation when I get this question is drawn directly from our benchmarking report we conduct each year. We look at a 12-month period that includes both live and on-demand events and webcasts. Data is gathered from 40,000 webcasts and events that enterprise, association, and media organization customers have run.

Based on our findings, as you can see in Figure 7.1, Wednesdays and Thursdays are the most popular days to host your virtual events. Let me tell you a little more about why: on Mondays people are focused on organizing their week and a lot of leadership and weekly team meetings are held on Mondays, so people have less time to focus on an event. On Fridays, many are trying to meet those end-of-week deadlines and honestly wrap up as early as possible to start their weekend.

The most popular time to start a virtual event continues to be either 7:00 a.m. Central Time, 9:00 a.m. Central, or 10:00 a.m. Central, as shown in Figure 7.2. In making the final determination on time, you need to look at where you think the bulk of your audience will come from. If most people will come in from the West Coast, then 10:00

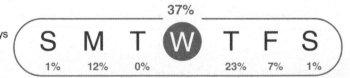

Most popular days to schedule a Virtual Event

S 1% · M 12% · T 0% · **W 37%** · T 23% · F 7% · S 1%

Virtual Events typically include 1-2 live days, followed by a 3-6 month on-demand period. Events that are scheduled for multiple days tend to start earlier in the week, with Wednesday being the most popular.

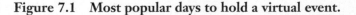

Figure 7.1   Most popular days to hold a virtual event.

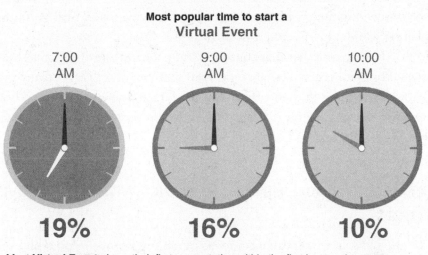

Most popular time to start a
Virtual Event

7:00 AM   9:00 AM   10:00 AM

19%   16%   10%

Most **Virtual Events** have their first presentation within the first hour and average **17 hours of content** with **an on-demand period of 6 months**. We are also seeing global customers scheduling their **Virtual Events** in a "follow-the-sun" format with unique timings for different regions to attract local audiences, influencing the average **Virtual Events** live period.

Figure 7.2   Most popular time to start an event.

a.m. Central will work best, as this translates to be the beginning of someone's day on the West Coast and your event still falls in the late morning for the Central and East Coast attendees.

In another scenario, if the majority of your audience is East Coast and EMEA, then 7:00 a.m. Central will be the best start time because East Coasters are just starting their day and it's midday in EMEA. My point is that you need to take the best practices and adapt them to your audiences.

Now you have to take your current agenda and think about how many of those sessions really fit with your main target audience. If this is your first event, you're going to want to be conservative with your sessions because you're going to need to manage all these speakers and onboard them into a new environment.

Determine how many days and/or sessions you want to host. I recommend having no more than six hours of programming per day. That's about the top end of daily programming that will allow people to balance watching content along with the work that is still going to pop up while they're at their desks.

Always remember that content is king. This is one of the areas that is key for the success of your event. Your audience has different viewing habits at home or in their office than they do at a physical event. They are also viewing on all different devices, computers, laptops, tablets, phones, and event TVs.

ENGAGING YOUR VIRTUAL AUDIENCE WITH INTERACTIVE TOOLS

Think about how you can a create as much interaction as possible.

I know if I was attending an industry conference, there are people I want to meet, so I will need tools to be able to reach out and set up one-on-one meetings.

These are some creative things that I have seen executed successfully across all audiences and event types:

- *College Reunion Locations* – Setting up virtual rooms for groups of people to meet up for chats who graduated from the same schools.

- *Online Poker* – I recently was told of a virtual conference where they streamed their key executives in a virtual poker tournament with some professional poker players with all the proceeds going to charity.

- *Use of Celebrities* – Having celebrities welcome you to the event or participate in a live chat or having a musical artist perform a private virtual concert just for your organization.

- *Attendee Selfies* – Have your attendees take a selfie or image and upload it to the virtual event board. This makes your audience feel like they are contributing to the program and it allows attendees to see who is at the event.

- *Scavenger Hunt* – Set up some time for your attendees to go on a virtual scavenger hunt. This is a great way to have a little fun with the audience and get them away from just watching content.

- *Virtual Wine Tasting* – You can enable attendees to order a set of three or four bottles of wine, or you can send them the wine and then bring on an amazing wine expert to conduct a virtual tasting with your audience. This is fun and educational and it is something that your audience will remember. Keep in mind this does not have to be wine; it can be a meal or desserts.

- *Magic Class* – Have a few five-minute magic breaks, where the master magician will teach your audience a few tricks that they can do on their own for their friends and family.

- *Comedy Session* – Bring in a comic and have a comedy break; this is another way to break up the day and nothing is better than a little laughter during a long day of sessions.

- *Movie Premiers* – Have a movie night where the audience can chat along with the movie. I have even heard of organizations bringing in the director or one of the stars of the movie for a Q&A following the viewing.

- *Award Shows* – Nothing is more fun than having a virtual awards show. You can make this your own version of the Oscars; your attendees can even vote on the winners.

- *Charitable Auctions* – Have an auction of some great items with the proceeds going to a charity of your choice.

- *Food Ordering* – Send your attendees a gift box for them to enjoy while they are attending the virtual event. Think popcorn and candies.

- *Gift Giving* – Don't forget everyone likes to receive a gift. So see how you can add it to your program.

Interactive Tools

Engaging your audience may seem like a difficult task but there are a number of interactive tools like gamification and theming that you will have at your disposal to help you create memorable virtual experiences.

These tools have been around as long as we've been holding meetings online. However, they've taken on an even greater importance as event organizers look for virtual replacements for in-person meetings.

Polls and Surveys

Use these to gauge understanding and keep your audience watching. Spread polls throughout individual sessions within your event and use surveys at the end of sessions to validate the impact of the content for your viewers. Our client benchmark study found that 79% of attendees respond to polls in live webcasts.

You should also have an all-encompassing event survey available for your attendees. This survey can be set up to appear at the end of the last session of your event. It can appear in the event navigation or you can set it to appear when the attendee clicks on the Exit link in the navigation to exit the event.

Chat

It's rare these days to attend a webcast or virtual event without there being a chat box. But are you making the most of this gem? Consider having event staff or members of your team "seed" the discussion with chat icebreakers, similar to what you would do for an in-person discussion, at the beginning of sessions to encourage viewers to chat along with the presentations they attend.

General Chat Icebreaker Examples

- "Where is everyone tuning in from today?"
- "Hi, I'm from [city], where is everyone else from?"

- "It's beautiful and sunny here in [city], what's the view out your window?"

- "I'm a [title] at [org name], what's your role and where do you work?"

- "What would everyone like to learn today?"

- "What do you expect to get out of this event/training/session?"

- "I'm excited to hear [speaker name]; has anyone else heard her?"

- "What are some of the challenges you guys are seeing with [topic name]?"

- "I can't wait to hear more about [topic]; what about all of you?"

- "I've been having a lot of success with [topic]; what's your experience?

Icebreaker Examples to Use During the Presentation (react to a soundbite from the speaker)

- "That stat was so interesting. I can relate because..."

- "I've had that exact same experience [provide example]..."

- "I've heard that before and it helped me to..."

- "I tried that method/approach and I had X outcome."

- "Wow, I can totally relate to X, what about all of you?"

- "I never knew that, did any of you?"

Q&A

Much like chat, these days it's much more common than not to have the ability to ask questions during an online session. But as we see the uptake of virtual events expanding exponentially, it's important to be aware of how many more questions you may receive on individual sessions. Including a moderator will help presenters vet and respond to the most important questions during the live event. I go into more detail on how to successfully engage a moderator a little later in this chapter.

Gamification

In all walks of life, we strive for reward, status, achievement, self-expression, competition, and altruism. Game mechanics can be used in virtual event platforms to drive engagement around these desires.

During physical events you'll most often see games used to encourage attendees to visit booths and drive overall traffic in the exhibit hall. One example of this from physical events that immediately comes to mind is "passport to prizes."

For "passport to prizes," you provide the attendee with a printed passport with a select number of companies listed and their booth numbers. When an attendee visits that booth, they will get a stamp in their passport. Once the attendee has all the stamps needed in the passport, the passport can be turned in to be entered in a random drawing for an array of prizes, typically done in the last 30 minutes or so of exhibit hall hours on the last day of the event.

You can replicate this same concept through badging or trivia. Here's how you do it:

Badges

Badges are an integral part of an attendee's user profile and provide a way for event planners to identify attendees or map out the attendee journey.

Activities can be assigned to badges to align with the event's goals and objectives. These actions are typically focused on driving attendees to engage with content. Sponsors can also create a badge that can be earned for visiting that company's booth and taking an action while there.

Tracking attendee progress through leaderboards in the environment to show the top performers can drive the competitive nature among attendees and tie it into your reward system.

In a virtual event, badges can be used to identify attendees or can be earned for a certain action or set of actions an attendee takes within the environment.

There are three types of predefined badges:

1. *Identification Badges* – This badge type is associated with a classification type such as Attendee Type, Sponsor Type, Sponsor User Type, and Space Type. It answers "Who I am."

2. *Credential Badges* – This badge type is a clarification of a user's role such as Speaker, Faculty, Press, Analyst, etc. It answers "What I am."

3. *Achievement Badges* – This badge type is earned based on a user's activity in an event, such as visiting host spaces, engaging in chat, and watching presentations. It answers "What I have accomplished."

These are some of the actions that you can drive through achievement badges:

- Complete a survey
- Ask a question
- Engage in a chat
- Accept a private chat
- Download a document from session handouts or a booth
- Visit a booth
- Complete your profile
- Answer a poll
- Log into the event over multiple days

Achievement badges can be based on having attendees engage in one action multiple times or package multiple actions together. Here are some examples:

- *Avid Reader* – Download 10 documents.

- *Content Commentator* – Participate in over 7 session chats.

- *Energizer* – Shared a session or the event on social media during the live day(s).

- *Gamer* – Completed trivia and earned more than 10 badges.

- *Profile Master* – Completed all profile information including uploading a photo.

- *Session Seeker* – Attended over 8 live or on-demand sessions.

- *Social Butterfly* – Participated in over 5 one-on-one chats, increasing their network reach.

- *Social Commentator* – Make over 8 posts in the lounge.

- *Voyager* – Visit nine booths for two minutes or more each and download nine pieces of content.

Trivia

There's nothing like a good round of trivia to test knowledge and bring out the competitive spirit! Adding trivia to your virtual event can help to encourage retention while engaging your attendees, especially between sessions or keynote presentations.

Trivia questions can relate to your event's theme, a product, your industry, or current events. Trivia can also serve as a practice test if you happen to be offering a certification or educational credits during your event.

Leaderboards

Here's where all those badges and trivia questions come together, as attendees can see their earned points in relation to other attendees. This not only encourages engagement but can help attendees connect with one another as they compete for bragging rights.

Here's an extra engagement checklist for success so that you can ensure your audience is active and not passive.

- Cross-promote on social media by tagging influencers and speakers in your posts and using event-related hashtags.

- Publish key takeaways to social media in real-time (e.g. live tweet) to create buzz. Dedicate a social media moderator on your team. Having an individual watching over all your channels and making timely updates can keep all your audiences engaged.

- Use in-event announcements to share content without leaving the event. For example, announce details of the latest prize or highlight the person at the top of the leaderboard.

Giveaways

One thing I've learned from physical events is that people go crazy about giveaways. These items are usually small and inexpensive but human nature drives us to want whatever everyone else has and that drives demand.

Giveaways are also another way to connect your speakers to the event experience. Speakers sometimes provide signed copies of their book, or if you have a keynote speaker who is a retired athlete, people will do anything to get a signed picture.

Just because your event is virtual doesn't mean you have to give up on giveaways. Many of my clients have just started to look at distribution in a new way.

Before the event it's easy to pull a list of attendees during the event or post-event, and send them a gift box, gift card, or a paper certificate of completion for an accredited course they took.

Here are some examples:

- A beverage client sent registrants samples of a new flavor of their drink to try before the event so everyone could provide their opinion in the lounge chat.

- A marketing client sent a branded gift box to key clients that were at the VP level and above that included a famous speaker's new book and a high-end coffee tumbler to get that executive group excited about attending the next day's keynote featuring the book's author. The keynote was at 9:00 a.m. so the tumbler was sent to hold their morning coffee.

- A technology client pulled attendee reports at two designated times in the day during their live event so that those people would get coffee gift cards to enjoy a coffee break the week after the event concluded.

THEMING YOUR EVENT

If you think about the context of a physical event, there is a common theme with branding elements used to pull everything together. From the tagline on the press release announcing the event to the branding on your delegate badges, to the décor of each breakout room, it's this theme that creates a cohesive experience.

Your virtual event can have all these elements but you can take it so much further because you aren't hindered by space, labor, or cost restrictions. We had one client that redesigned the lobby and one of the exhibit halls of their virtual event to look just like their gyms. To do this same thing at a physical event would add thousands of dollars to your budget and could potentially expose you to liability if someone were to injure themselves. In a virtual event, adding these theming elements only requires some additional creative hours to give it some soul.

Some ideas to consider as you look to bring your event together:

- *Personalization* – Naturally, your virtual event environment will be aligned from a branding perspective. But what if attendees saw you and your team when entering the lobby? Instead of stock photos, use photos of your team to welcome attendees when they first arrive at the virtual event.

- *Gamification* – We looked at the individual tactics in the previous section, but it bears noting that each of these elements can help reinforce your theme. Devise trivia questions and select badge names and icons that align with the theme of the event.

One of my favorite examples of successful theming is our virtual sales kickoff that my team did in 2020. Our theme was "Through the Decades." We assigned each sales team from around the globe a decade to dress up as and we pulled the theme through the webcast graphics, our badging, and our trivia. What really pulled it all together for our team was having everyone – presenters and attendees – dress up.

We saw incredible costumes from every decade and were treated to presentations from me as Axl Rose, the Fresh Prince, Kurt Cobain, and more. More than anything, all these great costumes and graphics was what set the chat on fire and what our sales teams are still talking about to this day!

Combine all these tactics together and you have something far greater than a "stand in" for your in-person event. Instead, you'll have created a true experience that captures the most salient elements of the in-person conference while adding unique virtual elements to connect and engage your attendees in a more meaningful and more measurable way.

PACKAGING CONTENT

Entering Your Event

First impressions matter, so pay special attention to what attendees see and hear when they first arrive. Your attendees will most likely be entering your event through the lobby and you want to make your opening as memorable as possible and keep things creative.

When you graphically design your lobby, you'll want to make sure that you make the areas that you most want attendees to visit, like your theatre and exhibit hall, be visible so that attendees have one easy click to important spaces.

I strongly advise that you include a welcome video in your lobby that plays the first time that any new attendee enters. Your welcome video should include a virtual host. This can be someone from your executive team, or most virtual event companies offer video production services and can provide you with a host.

The virtual host is a person, recorded via video, who welcomes attendees to the event.

Virtual hosts help provide a personal, multimedia-based welcome to attendees. The recorded greeting helps acquaint participants with the platform, the schedule for the day, and the main areas of the environment.

The virtual host can also provide attendees with a virtual tour of the space. The host should walk them through each area on the navigation bar and familiarize them with what will occur in each space and make them aware of any important functionality, like the fact that they have to log into a new webcast after each break, for example. The host will also explain when to use chat versus Q&A for technical support and how to use the briefcase.

Virtual hosts can also appear throughout the environment in different spaces and can introduce presentations with prerecorded or live introductions. Virtual hosts can be a great way to guide attendees through the event experience just like an MC.

How to Set Up Your Webcast Flow

Now that you have decided on the individual sessions you'll include in your agenda, we have to figure out how to package them. Referring to the benchmark study we conducted, we found that the average viewing time for a live 60-minute webcast is 46 minutes and for a 60-minute on-demand webcast, it's 31 minutes (see Figure 7.3).

Based on this data, scheduling shorter webcasts (from 30 to 45 minutes) may increase the average attendee view time and engagement.

Webcast View Time & Duration

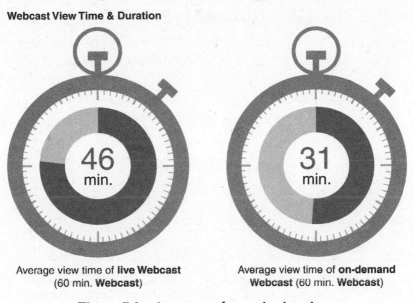

Average view time of **live Webcast** (60 min. **Webcast**)

Average view time of **on-demand** **Webcast** (60 min. **Webcast**)

Figure 7.3   Average webcast viewing time.

These are some options of how to best use the time in your webcast:

- 60 minutes (45 minutes of content with 15 minutes Q&A)

- 30 minutes (20 to 25 minutes of content with 5 to 10 minutes Q&A)

- 15 minutes (e.g. snackable content, customer stories, entertaining segments)

There are two main things that you have to take into consideration when you package your content.

The first is that webcast programming can be produced one of two ways, either as a constant flow of programming for a predetermined amount of time or as individual webcasts.

1. Constant Program Flow Webcasts

Pros:

- Attendees log into a webcast and can view content continuously for the duration of that webcast.

- Constant programming gives your program more of a TV broadcast feel.

- You're asking attendees to take fewer actions since they aren't clicking in and out of webcasts as often.

Cons:

- Prepare yourself for the challenge of coordinating all your speakers to be available at the same time and be patient as other speakers ahead of them complete their sessions. This will be true whether you prerecord your session or run it live.

One important thing to note with constant programming, whether it's prerecorded or live: you're going to need some kind of transition from one session or speaker to the next. If you simply pop speakers in and out of your scene without any explanation, your attendees can become easily confused, especially if they are coming in the middle of the program.

I recommend having a host who will be responsible for maintaining a consistent flow throughout the program. He or she is responsible for making a general introduction of the content block, introducing each speaker, closing the session once the speaker is done with his or her session, and the host will also handle a Q&A session, if you decide to include one. I'll go through how a host can successfully run a Q&A session just a little later in this chapter.

2. Individual Webcasts

Pros:

- You're only coordinating one speaker or group of speakers, if it's a panel, so scheduling a prerecorded or live session will be much less complex.

Cons:

- A webcast can be anywhere from 15 minutes to an hour long. Each time a webcast ends your attendees are going to have to close out of that webcast and click over to enter the next webcast.

- If your audience is not technology savvy, asking attendees to click in and out of webcasts so frequently may become incredibly frustrating for them and push them to abandon your programming.

Both options have their advantages but what I recommend is a combination of individual webcasts and a webcast that is a constant flow of programming. For example, you're going to want your keynotes to be their own webcast while your sessions, whether they are in tracks or not, should be longer constant flowing webcasts.

Here's a sample of how you can lay this out.

Day 1

TRACKS	A	B	C	D	E
12 p.m. PST	Keynote - Webcast 1				
12:30	Webcast 2	Webcast 3	Webcast 4	Webcast 5	Webcast 6
	30 min	30 min	30 min	30 min	30 min
	30 min	30 min	30 min	30 min	30 min
	30 min	30 min	30 min	30 min	30 min
2:00	BREAK				
	Webcast 7	Webcast 8	Webcast 9	Webcast 10	Webcast 11
	30 min	30 min	30 min	30 min	30 min
	30 min	30 min	30 min	30 min	30 min
	30 min	30 min	30 min	30 min	30 min
4:00	Lounge				

Examples of sessions that can be one of these webcasts include:

- Topical sessions
- Breakout sessions
- Workshops
- Training sessions
- Exhibit hall talks

Run of Show

You're going to have to pull all your webcasts together into a run of show so that your speakers, host, and the entire production team know exactly how the day is going to flow. Throughout the event, each team member should be following the document to ensure that scheduled activities are happening on time. Reference the run of show example in Figure 7.4 to build your event agenda. Once you have your agenda nailed down, be sure to include calendar invites in your email communications and event website so your attendees can block the time on their calendars.

- *Live Time* – Make sure you designate what time zone the show will be running in. I've seen teams that forget this important step and on the day of the show they find that part of their team has been waiting for an extra hour with nothing to do or is an hour or two late, which can cripple a program.

- *Session Title* – In this example it refers to the title of the session and it also refers to notes the host needs as he or she transitions from one session to the other.

DAY Live Time	Session Title	Speaker Name(s)	Sources (live people, pre-recorded video, image, etc.)	Slides for Session (Y/N)	Studio or Webcam	People in Session (in addition to Presenters)	Notes
8:00 AM - 8:05 AM	Welcome & Housekeeping (we can't go into solution selling without some more Mean Tweets)	Jane Smith	None	N	Webcam	None	
8:06 AM - 8:07 AM	Roll Mean Tweet Package 3	Pre-record	Pre-record	Pre-record	Pre-record	None	
8:08 AM - 8:48 AM	Solution Selling	Tom Anderson and Jerry Johnson	One short video clip	Y	Rajul in Studio/ Gerard on webcam		No PIP space on slides, so going to be slides + Rajul + Gerard the whole time
8:49 AM - 8:50 AM	Introduce case studies	Jane Smith	None	N	Webcam	None	
8:51 AM - 9:14 AM (23 min PRE-RECORD)	Client Success Stories, Part 2	Kyle and Doug - Clients: Karen and Lauren	Pre-rec'd	Pre-record	Pre-record	Pre-record	
9:15 AM - 9:17 AM	Close morning and transition to break but we can't leave you without another teleprompter challenge (Beck vs Sarah singing Wake me Up by Avicii) - with poll question	Jane Smith	None	N	Webcam	None	
9:18 AM - 9:19 AM	Roll Sarah vs Beck teleprompter challenge	Pre-record	Pre-record	Pre-record	Pre-record	None	
9:20 AM - 9:40 AM	BREAK						

Figure 7.4   Run of show example.

- *Speaker Name* – Designate who will be speaking, or if there is no speaker, just put "prerecorded."

- *Sources* – This refers to any assets that will be part of the webcast in addition to the speaker. This is where you note if the speaker includes a video as part of the session, a live guest as part of their session, or a static image.

- *Slides* – Indicate if the speaker will have a PowerPoint deck.

- *Studio or Webcam* – In this example the producer had some speakers using their computer webcams and others in a studio. The production team needs to know how the speaker will be coming into the production.

- *People in Session* – This is where you would indicate if a host would join the session at all; usually that would happen if the host were conducting live Q&A.

Determining Theatre Layout

Now that you've figured out how many webcasts you're going to have and which will be single and which will be a constant flow, you have to place them within your theatres. I call these theatres but that doesn't mean you have to. You can name this area whatever you'd like. If your attendees are used to seeing their session in an auditorium or speaker hall, you can easily change the name within your platform.

You can place all your sessions into one theatre. If you have tracks, each track will be a tab and attendees will click on the tab of the track they are interested in and then click on the webcast they want to attend (see Figure 7.5).

Your other option is to have multiple theatres and divide them by a topic, as shown in Figure 7.6. For example, you can divide your theatres this way:

- Theatre 1: Keynotes
- Theatre 2: Topic 1

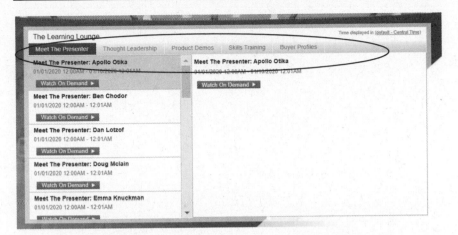

Figure 7.5   Single theatre with tabs example.

Figure 7.6   Multiple theatres example.

- Theatre 3: Topic 2

- Theatre 4: Topic 3

- Theatre 5: Exhibit Hall Talks

There's no right or wrong way to do this but the main factor in determining which route you take is the number of sessions you have. Here are a few examples:

Example #1: I have one keynote and eight 30-minute sessions

Theatre Buildout:
>You could run this event over one day
>Theatre 1: Keynote

>• Single Keynote webcast

>Theatre 2: Sessions
>2 two-hour webcasts with a break in between

Example #2: I have two keynotes and 12 one-hour sessions

You could run this event over one day if your sessions are running concurrently. If they are not, this event should be run over two days
>Theatre 1: All Keynotes – 2 single webcasts
>Theatre 2: 4 sessions under topic #1
>Theatre 3: 4 sessions under topic #2
>Theatre 4: 4 sessions under topic #3

Example #3: I have six keynotes and one hundred 45-minute sessions

This event would have to be run over multiple days even if your sessions run concurrently. With an event of this size it's a good idea to have a comprehensive agenda listed in your theatre as a drop-down so attendees can easily access all sessions across all days.

Theatre 1: All Keynotes

Theatre 2: 25 sessions under topic #1 with tabs breaking down the sessions into subcategories

Theatre 3: 25 sessions under topic #2 with tabs breaking down the sessions into subcategories

Theatre 4: 25 sessions under topic #3 with tabs breaking down the sessions into subcategories

Theatre 5: 25 sessions under topic #4 with tabs breaking down the sessions into subcategories

ADAPTING THE EXHIBIT HALL

We've got your agenda taken care of, so let's focus our attention on your exhibitors.

Although this is a virtual environment, exhibit halls are not built to hold an unlimited number of booths. Each exhibit hall lobby can accommodate about 15 to 20 booths. What that means is that graphically you can place 15 to 20 booths on that exhibit hall page without the booths being packed in too closely together, making it difficult for the attendee to decipher one from another or difficult to read listings to determine which booth belongs to which company.

Now you're wondering, what if I have more than 20 booths? Similar to my theatre examples above, if you have 20 or more booths, then you'll be able to place all those booths in the environment, but you will have multiple exhibit halls created for you that can be viewed in a drop-down menu.

Each exhibit hall lobby will look the same; the only difference will be the names of the booths in those exhibit halls. It's up to you to organize your exhibit halls in whatever way you think will make the most sense for your audience. Some examples I've seen work well are:

- Alphabetically by company name (e.g. A–C, D–F, G–J)
- By sponsorship level (e.g. the exhibit hall in your first drop-down is all platinum sponsor exhibitors, the next in the drop-down is gold sponsor exhibitors)
- By specialty area (e.g. analytics, finance, innovation)
- By company physical location (e.g. United States, Scandinavia, Central America)

Virtual Booth Build-Out

With a physical event, once your exhibitor pays for their space, they order services, coordinate shipping and labor, and it falls on them to get their booth to your location. For a virtual event, there is much more coordination that your internal team is going to have to do to prepare your exhibitor companies.

In a virtual event, each booth will have to be built out and you'll need to conduct training for those who will be working at the booth during the live days.

Booths in your virtual event can be customized to reflect the branding of each company. The actual build-out process takes about 15 to 20 minutes per booth, but this can add up quickly based on the number of booths that need to be built. Booths can be built out either by you, by the event host, or by each of the exhibiting companies.

Event Host Builds the Booth
Pros:

- Booth build-outs most likely will happen more quickly because one or a group of people on your team are solely responsible for meeting the booth building deadline.

- Direct contact with the virtual event vendor makes it easy to get questions answered quickly.

Cons:

- Depending on how many booths need to be built, this is a time-consuming process that may require additional staff.

- You'll need to factor in time to allow all your exhibitors to get you all the assets they would like displayed in their booth as well as any branding elements like logos and colors.

- You will need to factor in time in your process to set up individual or group sneak previews so exhibitors can view and approve their booths. Be prepared for about 50% or more exhibitors to have updates or changes that will require more of a time investment from your staff.

Exhibiting Company Builds the Booths

Pros:

- The exhibiting company is responsible for gathering all their own booth assets and allocating a person to build out the booth.

- Less of a time commitment from your team.

Cons:

- Individual or group trainings will need to be set up for exhibitors.

- Expect to be fielding a lot more questions and being asked to be part of team calls to walk through any booth-building issues.

- Be prepared for exhibitors not to meet the build-out deadline. When setting your deadline determine a date about four days before the event's drop-dead booth build-out date to account for exhibitors who will ask for more time.

Virtual Booth Customizations

As I mentioned, each booth can be customized for the exhibiting company and reflect that company's branding, logo, and general look and feel. These are the areas that you'll be able to customize when you build out your booth:

- *Booth Name* – Name your booth, usually this will be your company name. Your booth name will be displayed in the event's directory of sponsors.

- *Booth Style* – Allows you to choose the visual appearance of your sponsor space. Space styles are chosen for aesthetic value and to match your corporate image. Each style offers identical functionality.

- *Booth Colors* – Choose the primary and secondary colors of your booth tabs. Primary will apply to tab backgrounds, secondary will apply to font color. You will need to know the hex value of the colors you choose (i.e. #XXXXXX). You should be able to get this information from your marketing or design department.

- *Booth Logo* – This step allows you to upload your sponsor space logo, which is typically your company logo. Generally, accepted file types include .gif, .jpg, .png, or .swf.

- *About Us Section* – Tell us about your company. Avoid using special characters (%, &, *, $, @, (), ""). A best practice is to keep this text under 250 characters, including spaces.

- *Front Screen Welcome Image/Video* – This step allows you to add animations, presentations, graphs, and short video clips to your sponsor space. The optimal size for an image is 484 × 272 px (.jpg, .png files) and preferably under 10MB for video file (.mp4, .mov, .avi, .flv, .wmv).

- *Documents and Links* – Upload all downloadable content that you would like available for attendees here. This typically includes links to your corporate website, brochures, product guides, whitepapers, etc. You may upload almost any type of file, but best practice is to stick with .pdf files.

- *Tab Content* – All of the document links that you want to include in your booth are organized in tabs. Booths are usually set up with the following standard tabs: Documents and Links, Message Board, Video Collection, External URL, Live Chat, Social Media Feeds, and Survey. You may change the verbiage and display order of the tabs. There is generally a 10-tab limit in all booths.

- *Video Collection* – Think of this as your own YouTube channel. Feel free to upload an unlimited number of videos here. File size limit is usually 10MB per video file.

- *Marquee Message* – This is a rolling ticker in your booth. This message is typically used to add a welcome message, highlight a special product/deal/promotion, or make an important announcement. A best practice is to keep this short and sweet; one sentence will suffice. There is usually a limit of one message per booth.

- *Staff* – You can add the names and contact information of all your employees who will be working the booth. Your staff members should fully complete their online profile in the environment so that attendees have all the information they need to contact them during and after the event.

- *Search Words* – Insert keywords associated to your booth and content to make your space more searchable throughout the virtual environment. A best practice is to separate each word/phrase with a comma only, no spaces.

LOUNGES

Lounges are a centralized area within your event where you can drive attendees to engage in group chats. It's the equivalent to a physical event networking lounge. Many virtual events have a functionality that shows you who is in the lounge at a given time so you can spot anyone whom you might want to connect with.

You can invite your speakers to be in the lounge at a given time and promote that to attendees so that they can interact with the speaker to ask follow-up questions from the Q&A session, inquire about a new topic, or just tell them how much they liked their session.

You can also have multiple lounges and designate lounges by industry or area of expertise. You could have one lounge just for your engineers or another lounge just for store managers.

RESOURCE CENTERS

The resource center is your one-stop-shop for any materials and handouts from the event. You can place any handouts from speakers and anything that you as the event host want to share.

However, do not put any of your exhibitor's materials in this space. You want to make sure that attendees are visiting each exhibit booth to get those materials.

Now that you have your content all aligned, you have to make sure that your speakers are comfortable and ready to present. Our next chapter provides some detailed best practices and tips on how to get your speakers ready to present on camera.

CHAPTER 8

Preparing Speakers for Virtual Appearances

F or people used to presenting to an in-person audience, speaking to a 100% virtual audience can be challenging. You can't make eye contact with your audience or read body language. You're looking directly at the small circle that's the lens of your webcam. You may wonder if anyone can even hear you.

The content management lead should provide speakers with training and guidance on the virtual event platform and teach them how to best present to a virtual audience.

In this chapter, I'll provide best practices and tips to prepare speakers to present on a webcam or in front of a professional camera at a hybrid event.

PROVIDING SPEAKERS A "STUDIO IN A BOX"

With so many presenters now presenting from their homes or home offices, often they don't know what equipment they should be using.

If your speaker will be working with you long term, send them a "mini-studio in a box":

- A small step and repeat to use as a background. A step and repeat is a branded background that you usually see people taking pictures in front of. The name comes from the fact that you stand in front of it, get your picture taken or give your interview, and then the next person literally steps in and repeats the same action. The smaller step and repeats are about 7'×10' and come in packaging about the size of a carry-on bag.

- A ring light – these lights are actual rings that are about 18 inches in diameter. They can sit on the table in front of the presenter and provide more light for a higher quality look on video.

- If you don't want speakers using earbuds, you can order them a USB lapel microphone that connects to your collar and gives you a cleaner look when presenting.

- Computer webcams nowadays are really high quality but if you have a speaker with an older computer or no webcam, which is rare, you can also send your speaker a higher-quality webcam that is USB plug and play.

SPEAKER READINESS COMMUNICATIONS

These are the steps you need to take to get your speakers ready to present in a virtual event:

- Prepare an onboarding email welcoming the speaker to the event and that provides the following information:

  - Explain how the agenda is structured.

  - Confirm the day and time of the speaker's session and the session format (single speaker, panel, etc.).

  - Outline the length of the session and how Q&A will be handled. If this hasn't been finalized yet, that's okay; let them know that you are working on this and more information is to follow.

  - Lay out any content-related deadline dates and what he or she can expect from you in the coming weeks.

- Set up a technical check with the speaker before the live day or before they record their presentation.

This is an imperative step because it allows your webcast engineer to troubleshoot technical issues and also recommend any equipment that will improve the quality of the presentation. This technical check will also be the first time your speaker will see the back end of the webcast tool so part of the technical check should be to educate the speaker on how Q&A will look and be handled, how slides will be advanced, and how speakers will be brought in and out of the scene based on the session flow.

- Finalize all speaker assets and set a timeline to receive these.

    Speakers should have the ability to provide handout documents and links; push out live polling questions and real-time answers from the audience; integrate videos, slides, or images as part of their session; and have an end-of-session survey.

BEST PRACTICES FOR ON-CAMERA INTERVIEWS

The purpose of the interview is to build a personal connection with the audience. The speaker can use this to his or her advantage in terms of how his or her personal brand is presented. Reading slides verbatim or using a teleprompter for an hour presentation doesn't give any room for the speaker's personality to shine through.

Embrace and Understand the Nature of Live

- Do not strive for perfection
- "Keep it real" to better connect
- Avoid reading to the audience

Have Some Perspective

In the whole scheme of life, this is but a small moment in time. Put things in perspective, take a breath, and go for it. It will be over before you know it.

Being Nervous Isn't Always a Bad Thing

Plain and simple, nervousness shows that this is important. This is a good thing! We have a tendency to feel blasé about things we aren't into or don't see the value/importance of doing. It is good to put care and effort into being in front of the camera.

You Are the Expert

Remind your speaker she was asked to do this interview because she has important and valuable information to share with others. In most cases, she knows the material better than anyone else so use that fact to boost your speaker's confidence!

Be Your Authentic Self

Let your speaker's authentic-self shine through; encourage them to be expressive and energetic. Even nervous laughter shows that they are "real." If they bumble a word, advise them not to make the "Oh, no!" face – just keep going. Chances are that the audience won't notice.

Practice, Practice, Practice

Practicing multiple times allows speakers to be able to make better eye contact with the camera (the audience) and gives them the confidence to take and pose questions throughout the interview.

Knowing Your Material Is Only Half the Picture

- Looking good and feeling good
- Creating "Zen-like" surroundings
- Rehearsing and seeking feedback from peers
- Be yourself

Advise speakers to wear something that is comfortable and they feel good about. Tell them that having a glass of water nearby, closing themselves off from distractions, and making sure the temperature of the room is comfortable are all little things that will make the environment more relaxed. Most importantly, make sure they have a few rehearsals under their belt to give them the ultimate confidence.

Setting Up and Framing Your Video

Don't have a fancy studio? By making minor adjustments, speakers can up the production value of their webcam presentations.

Centered and Less Headroom

When most people sit down in front of a webcam, they position themselves so their head is smack dab in the middle of the screen and then there's too much empty space above their head. In industry-speak, there's too much headroom.

Headroom refers to the amount of space between the top of the head and the top of the frame. Put too much and you'll look small and insignificant. Put too little (or none) and it will look like your head is stuck to the top of the screen.

Raise the Camera Up to Eye Level

Low camera angles are not flattering to anyone—they just make your speaker's face look jowly and distorted (and who wants that?).

The solution is simple: bring that webcam up to eye level, or even slightly above. Try stacking a few books underneath a laptop, or lowering the chair.

Light It Right

The only thing worse than an unflattering camera angle is not being able to see the speaker's face at all. This can happen when a window or bright light is behind the speaker—they become backlit. If possible, have them position their computer so they are facing a window to take advantage of the natural light coming in.

If there's no window or it's dark outside, turn on some lights. Overhead lights are better than none, but this kind of lighting isn't always flattering. A better solution, if the speaker is at home, have them set a lamp on either side of their computer to provide a soft, even light.

Simplify the Background

Messy closets. Cluttered bookshelves. Laundry on the couch. Friends and family may not care, but if your speaker is hosting a webcast, they should clean up that space.

You want people to focus on your speaker, not what's going on behind them. So advise them to keep the background as simple and uncluttered as possible.

If they are using a laptop, they have a lot of flexibility to move around and experiment with different locations. Choose a clean, bright wall. Avoid bookshelves or walls with lots of paintings or posters. Close any doors that might be in the background.

BEST PRACTICES FOR GUESTS

Before the Interview

Before any interview make sure to know the purpose. Prepare two or three essential points to get across during the interview and support those points with facts or anecdotes from experiences. Consider the interview an "extended conversation," so speak naturally.

During the Interview

Smile at the interviewer to establish a rapport. It's important to use vocal variety. Your speaker's voice and delivery reflect the full spectrum of emotions and points of emphasis. It's also acceptable to use gestures that complement the expression of ideas and communicate total enthusiasm and involvement in the subject. Maintain eye contact throughout the interview and keep an "open," friendly face.

Getting Your Point Across

The first step is to listen carefully to the question. If it is considered difficult, the speaker can pause before answering to give himself time to formulate a response. If he doesn't understand a question, he can ask that it be repeated.

The speaker should treat your host and the audience as they would friends and be friendly, spontaneous, and responsive. If it is a brief interview, condense the answers citing main points quickly; basically think in terms of an outline. Use analogies whenever possible to simplify main points, and where appropriate, relate personal experiences or illustrations of personal work to support statements. Telling audiences something personal will "humanize" the speaker to the audience. Many interviewers end interviews by asking if they have covered everything or if there is anything else the speaker would like to share. This is when the speaker can seize this opportunity to reinforce key points or takeaways or share something extra – this is a chance to end the conversation with the main topic or idea the audience should remember.

BEST PRACTICES FOR INTERVIEWERS/MODERATORS

A good anchor or a host is the one who drives the show and holds it all together. Whether you use a professional host or someone within your organization, here are some tips to share with him or her.

Wardrobe

Since an emcee keeps the show going and has a lot of stage time, her or his attire should be in accordance with the show being hosted. If your guests are casual, it's okay to also have a casual look.

Confident

You want to get the audience's energy as high as possible. Make sure you're smiling and that you sound genuine.

Well Prepared

An anchor should do his or her homework. Get the agenda well before the event, research the industry and speakers, and practice the script if necessary. Keep filler content ready for sticky situations.

Be Flexible

Last-minute changes are bound to happen. Chaos will ensue if the host fails to adapt to these changes properly. Remember that the audience is oblivious to the proceedings of the show. Take advantage of the very same fact and adjust the event accordingly. If you are co-hosting the show, then coordination with your partner is very important.

Being Familiar with the Broadcast

Be sure your host masters the set environment(s) (know the technology, who the go-to production staff members are, etc.). The host should review the guest list and double-check all pronunciations and ask the director for any notes. Be sure that they request that the set have several bottles of room-temperature water, tissues, pens, and Post-its. They should be sure to stay hydrated during breaks.

Dressing for On-Camera Success

When you are on camera, what you wear matters as much as the content you are presenting. The camera reacts differently to certain colors and patterns. Following these simple guidelines will ensure that your speaker is camera-ready to go on air.

What to Wear

Blues/Cooler Tones

Blue and other cool color tones enhance presenters on camera.

Tie Long Hair Back

Hair can interfere with the microphone and cause unwanted noises.

Contact Lenses

If possible, avoid glasses because they can cause glare. If contacts aren't an option, make sure to adjust lighting.

Makeup

Foundation helps both men and women avoid looking too shiny or washed out.

What Not to Wear

Small Patterns (e.g. polka dots)

Patterns can create interference with the camera, known as a Moire effect, that creates ripples on screen.

Busy Colored Patterns

Large patterns and too many colors can be distracting for viewers and take away from your message.

High Contrast (White, Black, Mixed)

High contrast between colors can make it hard for a camera to get the right tone.

Scarves

Same as hair, scarves can cause interference with the microphone.

Dangling Earrings and Shiny Jewelry

These accessories will reflect poorly under the harsh lights and cause a glare.

BEST PRACTICES FOR PRESENTING USING A MOBILE PHONE

More and more virtual platforms are offering the option for speakers to present right from their mobile phones. Presenting from a mobile phone is slightly different than presenting on a webcam. These are some tips that your speakers should be aware of that are specific to presenting on a mobile phone.

Use Landscape Orientation

Nothing ruins great footage like having two black vertical bars along both sides of your video. Avoid this mistake by making sure to use landscape orientation and not portrait orientation while recording.

Not only does landscape make the video more aesthetically pleasing in general but it will capture more in the actual video.

Stay Steady

To avoid having the video footage become distorted, blurred, or affected by "rolling shutter" the best thing to do is to keep the phone steady while recording. Use both hands to hold the smartphone as close as possible to the body as the video is being recorded or ask a friend to record the video. These are also great tools that can help:

- Stabilizers, tripods, and camera cages keep your smartphone or mobile device still when taking a video.

- If a smartphone tripod or stabilizer is not accessible, rest the phone on other physical supports like tables, chairs, desks, shelves, etc.

Ensure Good Audio

Shoot the video in a quiet place, preferably indoors when possible with less ambient noise.

For exceptional quality videos with superb audio, get an external recording device or at least a directional microphone that will work with a smartphone. If using an external microphone isn't possible or practical, then stay as close to the audio source as possible and try this little trick: have your speaker use their hand to cover around the phone's microphone (but don't completely cover it). This way, unwanted noise can be reduced.

Framing Faces

Use the rule of thirds: position the eyes about one third of the way from the top of the frame. The eyes are the center of attention in face shots. The speaker's headroom should be about 10% of the total height of the shot. The closer the shot, the less headroom there will be; crop out the top of the head rather than the chin if cropping is necessary.

Good Lighting Is Critical

Proper lighting has a huge impact on smartphone cameras because they have smaller image sensors and lenses. Try as much as possible to shoot video in brightly lit areas. This will help avoid unnecessary shadows and grainy areas in your video.

Conversely, be aware not to point the camera directly at bright light sources, which will cause unusable overexposed footage and lens flaring.

We've got your speakers trained and given them all the tools they need to look and feel great on camera. So now it's time for Lights, Camera, and Action! Let's shift our focus to your exhibitors and sponsors. In the next chapter, I'll show you how you can drive revenue through your virtual event.

CHAPTER 9

Monetization through Exhibitors and Sponsorships

My favorite phrase when it comes to sponsorships is "If it's customizable, it's monetizable!"

There are just as many ways to monetize your virtual environment and activities within that environment as with a physical event. What's more, the data you can provide them on all these assets is going to be much more robust than anything they could receive onsite.

In this chapter, I'll show you which virtual event groups can be new revenue streams, what elements in the event are monetizable, and how to build and price sponsorship packages in the virtual world.

WHAT ARE YOUR POTENTIAL REVENUE STREAMS?

Let's start out by looking at the three revenue streams you could potentially get from your audience: attendees, exhibitors, and sponsors.

Attendees

There is still an opportunity to generate revenue from attendees, but you won't be able to charge the same as you would for a physical event. There's just too much free digital content out there to justify a high event attendee fee. We've seen clients be most successful charging anywhere from $49 to $199. Attendees will be willing to pay the higher price point if the speaker lineup includes industry leaders, a celebrity speaker (think past presidents or sports figures), or very niche content.

The other option to drive higher registration fees is to offer educational credit or an industry certification. When you include these options, we've seen clients charge upwards of $600 to $2,000. I recently saw a large consulting firm conduct a multiday event that had over 2,500 attendees each paying over $2,000 for access to the event; they also included a celebrity speaker and a well-known recording artist to keep their audience engaged.

Exhibitors

To take advantage of this revenue stream you need to make sure you include virtual exhibit booths as part of your event. In order to tier the exhibit booth offerings, I wouldn't spend a lot of time making some exhibit booths look bigger or different than others, like in a physical exhibit hall. Instead you should tier the value of the booth by the type of functionality that the exhibitor has in the booth space. Examples include limiting the number of videos that can be uploaded in a booth, the ability to have one-on-one video chats, the number of marketing documents that can be included, or limiting the amount of data exhibitors can receive across exhibit booth tiers.

Sponsors

Virtual event sponsorships are where you can get most creative with your offerings, and if you have a hybrid event, that will provide you with even more sponsorship inventory when you package live and virtual sponsorship opportunities together.

PRICING EXHIBITOR BOOTHS AND SPONSORSHIPS—SOME CONSIDERATIONS

One of the first questions we usually get from clients is, how do I price my booths and sponsorships? For starters it's not apples to apples.

If you're used to charging $75,000 for a premium physical event sponsorship, you're not going to get that in the virtual world. But on the flipside you also don't have all those hard costs associated with a physical event, so you have to calculate your margins accordingly.

Each of my clients is different and determining pricing will depend on a number of variables that need to be taken into account, including the margin you want to hit after you've subtracted all your virtual event costs, the number of days your event will run, the number of attendees you expect, and price points you think your market will bear.

I've seen similar event build-outs in the tech industry charge double the price for sponsorships than in the beauty industry because the tech industry target audience were midsized corporations while the target audience for the beauty industry were single proprietors. Our beauty industry client made up their cost in sponsor and exhibitor volume while the tech client had fewer companies that paid more.

A good place to start is to consider these questions and recommendations:

- What amount of revenue do you expect to receive through all your virtual event revenue streams?

- Are your events well received and do you have a strong brand presence in your industry?

- How is the industry you are targeting performing? Do your sponsorship prospects have the money to spend?

- Is volume or exclusivity more important to you? Do you want to sell more sponsorships that are affordable or a few with premium pricing?

- Consider charging a 10% to 15% premium for audience quality over your fixed virtual event costs.

- Consider another 15% of your fixed costs for the fixed value you provide through facilitating the event.

Also remember that with a virtual event the sponsorship visibility does not end after the program does. If your virtual environment is going to be available for archive viewing of all the content, then everyone who logs in to watch the archives will see your sponsors' information, too.

EVENT FUNCTIONALITY THAT CAN BE CUSTOMIZED FOR SPONSORSHIPS

When you build out your sponsorship packages you need to start by evaluating all the functionality that your virtual event platform offers. This section breaks down all the areas within the virtual event that can be customized for a sponsor and included in a sponsorship package.

Display Ads

Your virtual event will have a number of spaces that may include your lobby, and one or multiple theatres, exhibit halls, and resource centers. Display ads will be available to you throughout all these spaces in a variety of sizes within the templates you are provided, and most times there will also be opportunities to customize your spaces to allow for more inventory.

Most if not all of these display ad spaces will rotate, which will give you a larger volume of ad inventory that can be offered. Depending on the size of your event, you may have multiple spaces, like multiple exhibit halls or theatres, which will again add to your inventory.

Display ads can be hyperlinked to the sponsor's website, a landing page, or virtual booth. You can decide as part of your sponsorship tier whether the hyperlinks in display ads will be activated.

Let me give you an example of how display ad inventory can add up: if you have two banner ads available in each exhibit hall and each banner ad has a maximum of 15 rotations, your display ad inventory in that space is 30. Now say your event will have 3 exhibit halls, that gives you 90 display ads that are available to package up.

One word of caution: just because you have all this inventory doesn't mean you should necessarily use it. You want to be sure to strike a creative balance between the number of sponsorship display ads and your branding throughout the environment. You always want to make sure that attendees can tell that this is your event.

Commercials and Video Advertising

Just like display ads, your virtual event will have some areas where you can run sponsor videos or commercials. You can offer multiple sponsors the opportunity to run commercials in select spaces exclusively or edit multiple sponsor commercials together to create one multi-sponsor package.

In the real world 30 seconds or a minute is not a lot of time at all, but in the world of video advertising, it's a lifetime. Advise your sponsors that commercials should be limited to 30 seconds to one minute at the longest. Think about your attention span when watching TV; you're not going to sit and digest over one minute of advertising no matter how interesting the product is.

Based on where commercials and video ads are in your environment, you can set them to auto-play the first time that an attendee enters that space, be on a constant loop in the space, or set them as "click to play" so the virtual event platform could track the number of video views.

Webcasts or Session Tracks

Just like sponsoring a track at a conference, you can sponsor virtual event content with a number of options:

Individual Webcast Speaking Opportunities

I find that the easiest content sponsorship to sell is going to be your speaking opportunity. Companies who buy this type of sponsorship will have a wide roster of executives that are seasoned speakers and when companies pay for a speaking slot they are going to provide a speaker who is as comfortable in front of a crowd as they are on camera.

I can't emphasize enough that you reassure your speaker that this shouldn't be just a talking head over slides session. The virtual event platform should provide the speaker with the ability to bring in prerecorded videos, images, and animations as well as one or more co-presenters.

Webcasts provide the speaker with the opportunity to include handouts and links that they reference or that support their topic. Speakers can also push out live polls, ask people to answer questions through the chat, or take questions through text-based Q&A and answer them at the end of the session. Best of all, if the speaker doesn't get to your question, they can be provided with a report of all questions and who asked them so that the speaker can reply to you personally after the session or event ends.

All of these options I've just described will capture multiple data points that would be difficult, if not impossible to capture during a live speech. Speakers can see how many people interacted with their polls and who those people were, see how many people attended their session down to the individual level, and also will know who downloaded their handouts.

Session Tracks

In addition to single-session speaking sponsorships, you can offer a company the ability to contribute to build out the content of one of your tracks. This can include giving that company input on the agenda build-out, choosing speakers, and having their executives speak.

Track sponsorships also provide options for branding and visibility through recognition in the theatre space and video pre-rolls that can run before your session starts, similar to "walk in" slides in a physical event.

Speaking Opportunity Inventory Analysis

When you're determining how many speaking opportunities to offer, you have to balance the amount of sponsored content you offer with the non-sponsored content.

First and foremost, sponsors should be coached that their speaking session is not a chance for them to deliver a product commercial. One of the reasons people attend events is to listen to content that will help them solve a problem, overcome a challenge, or learn how a peer in the industry achieved success. If sponsors start offering "salesy" sessions, you're going to see your attendance numbers drop quickly. Sponsors who present case studies, research findings, or co-present with a customer attract higher numbers of engaged attendees.

Now back to that balance between sponsor content and other industry-centric content. Attendees didn't come to just see sponsors speak; they want to hear from you as well as other dynamic speakers they can learn from. With all that in mind, I recommend that you use the 60/40 rule: allow no more than 40% of your content to be sponsored and the remaining 60% are your hand-picked speakers.

Content Inventory Case Study

In order to begin to do your inventory analysis, you're going to need a few crucial pieces of information:

- What is your speaking sponsorship revenue goal? Remember, this is the revenue you just want to make off the speaker sponsorships, not total revenue for the event.

- Length of time your content program will run (e.g. four hours of content per day for two days, three hours of content in one day)

- How many minutes each speaking session will be.

- What is the price of your sponsorship?

In the example I'm going to use, we know the following;

- My speaking sponsorship revenue goal is $61,000.

- I have a total of four hours of programming over two days.

- I have four sponsorship packages ranging from $4,500 to $10,000, and these opportunities allow my sponsors anywhere from 7 minutes to 17 minutes of speaking time.

In order to achieve my 60/40 content balance, I cannot allow any more than 96 minutes of sponsored speaker programming over two days.

When you plug all this data in it's going to look like this.

Participation Opportunities	Single Interview ($4.5K)	Single Interview Premium ($6.5K)	Panel Interview ($7.5K)	Track Sponsor ($10K)	Grand Total
Programming Time	7 minutes	10 minutes	10 minutes	17 minutes	
Opportunities Available	7	2	1	1	11
Meet Revenue Goal $61,000	$31,500	$13,000	$7,500	$10,000	$62,000
Total Run Time (TRT) of each package	49 minutes	20 minutes	10 minutes	17 minutes	96 minutes

Programming Inventory	Content Run Time (Day 1)	Content Run Time (Day 2)	Total Content Run Time (Days 1-2)	Total Content Percentage - Based on 4 Hours of Newsdesk
Sponsored Content	48 minutes	48 minutes	1 hour/36 minutes	40%
Editorial Content	1 hour/12 minutes	1 hour/12 minutes	2 hours/24 minutes	60%

I don't want you to think it just laid out perfectly on the first try. Your data points need to start with your best educated guess on how you want to get to your revenue goal. After you plug all your numbers in you're going to have to do some tweaking. I recommend that you make most of your adjustments at the sponsorship cost and number of opportunities available levels to get to your revenue goal because those two points are going to be the most flexible parts of your model. You're most likely not going to be able to lower your revenue goal or the length or your programming.

Website Recognition

As with a physical event, your company website will be the first place people will go to get information on your event, including date and time, schedule, speaker bios, registration information, and more.

There are a number of areas on the microsite where you can promote your sponsors, including:

- A sponsor page listing that may include information about the sponsor company and products or services.

- Prime location on the home page where you can feature sponsor logo visibility. I would not recommend having these logos hyperlinked because you do not want to distract visitors from your microsite's main call to action.

- Registration page – your registration page can be on your microsite or it can be an independent page that visitors can click to from the microsite. Sponsor logos can also appear on the registration page but again, don't make them clickable, the main call to action is to register.

- Login page – your login page is the way that your attendees will access the event. Sponsor logos and messaging can be featured on this page.

Email Communications

You are going to have two types of email campaigns when promoting your event: the first will be the campaign you build for prospects and the second is the campaign built for registrants.

There are a number of different options for sponsors in email communications, including:

- Sponsor logo visibility in the footer or sidebar of all emails, or you can divide your sponsors so one group gets visibility in prospect emails and the other gets visibility in registrant emails.

- Provide sponsors with a short one- or two-sentence paragraph at the end of your attendee emails that promotes the sponsor's speaking session or why attendees should visit the sponsor's booth.

- Put the sponsor's speaking session front and center as the main copy of the email. With this option it's important to emphasize that the messaging needs to focus the session content and not have a sales slant.

Gamification

The two most common gamification options that you will see in a virtual event are trivia games and badging.

Badging can be an effective tool for generating and sustaining attendee engagement and fostering connections but the value to sponsors is that badging drives attendees to perform specific actions.

Trivia games provide sponsors with a different vehicle that they can use to push out educational information or reinforce the information that was presented during sessions.

Trivia Games

Trivia games are fun and straightforward. Provide a number of trivia questions that relate to your industry, event theme, or topic – or questions that are just plain fun. Attendees earn points based on how many questions they get right and how quickly they answer correctly. Events have a leaderboard so people can see where they rank compared to their peers.

Trivia offers a few different sponsorship options; you can offer sponsors the ability to customize one or multiple questions that relate to their product or service or sponsor visibility can be placed on the trivia page (e.g. "Trivia brought to you by..."). You can also offer options for messaging on the opening trivia graphic or a welcome video introducing the trivia game. Any prizes can also be provided by the sponsor and they can even have the option to announce the winner at their booth.

Badging

Attendee achievement badges are a great way to encourage engagement and participation in an event as well as a healthy level of competition.

The real value that badges offer to sponsors is that earning badges is all based on actions within the platform that you assign and attendees need to complete to earn points and qualify for that badge.

Examples of these actions include:

- Accept a one-on-one text chat
- Accept one-on-one video chats
- Download assets from a sponsor booth
- Complete surveys or polls
- Attend a session or track
- Participate in a group chat
- Length of time you remain in the booth
- Booths visited

Sponsors can create their own badges and include their own graphic icon for the badge as well as assign specific actions that drive attendees to their particular booth and encourage them to take actions like initiate a chat or download a whitepaper.

Badging also comes with a leaderboard so attendees can track their progress and see how they are stacking up to their peers. With badging, sponsors can also sponsor one or multiple prizes for top point earners that can be announced and given away at the sponsor booth.

Marquee Messaging

Many virtual event environments have marquee messaging options, which refers to the scrolling ticker at the bottom of the screen similar to what you probably see often in TV news programs.

These messages can be customized to your sponsor and messages can change every day. The advantage of marquee messages is that they rotate throughout the event and can be scheduled to appear at specific times. The big value here is that no matter where you are in the event, you're going to see the marquee message. In the lobby, you're seeing it, move to the exhibit hall, you still see it, and so forth for each space.

Again, a word of caution to balance the sponsor messages with your own messaging as the event owner. This is your event and you have to make sure you direct attendees to actions that achieve your business objectives and goals.

Pop-Up Announcements

A pop-up announcement is a text-based announcement that literally "pops up" in the virtual event environment. These announcements are often used to alert attendees about upcoming sessions, updates to the agenda, or changes in session times.

Pop-up announcements are valuable to sponsors because they can also be customized and used to drive attendees to a sponsor booth, remind them of a sponsor's upcoming speaking session, prompt them how to earn a sponsor's badge, and much more. Pop-up announcements can be timed so you can work with your sponsor to strategically time announcements when attendees are more likely to be paying attention or looking for guidance, usually at the end of a session, at the end of the dedicated exhibit hall time, or right before a lounge chat.

As far as pop-up announcement inventory goes, you can stack pop-up announcements so that multiple announcements show up at one time. I recommend no more than four announcements at one time; otherwise attendees will be overwhelmed by so many messages and simply decide to not read any.

As the event host, you also need to control how many times pop-up announcements will be shown over the course of the day. If you push too many, it's going to start to be an annoyance. The best times to consider having pop-up announcements include:

- Anywhere from two minutes before to the end of a session block

- At the end of a break or dedicated exhibit hall time

- Anywhere from two minutes before to the beginning of a session block

- One or two times during the dedicated exhibit hall time

BUILDING OUT SPONSORSHIPS

Now that you know what options and virtual event functionality are monetizable, you can start to put together your sponsor packages using these best practices. Creating sponsorship packages is more art than science, so let's start with some tips and examples.

Tiered Options

Sponsorship programs should not be a one-size-fits-all option. You want to drive revenue, but you don't want to alienate any prospects. Even if you are focused on capturing a smaller number of sponsors at higher price points, you still want to offer a variety of price points. There are only so many companies with deep pockets and you're competing with other events for those dollars.

I've found that the easiest way to start to build out your tiers is to build out the one that has the most benefits and is the most expensive first. Add in everything you think that big-spending sponsor will ever want. Most likely you'll only sell one or two of these at the most.

As you tier down, all you do is peel away benefits from each package until you get to an exhibitor-only package.

Create a clear delineation between package tiers

In short, as you tier down your packages take out enough to ensure sponsors see a clear difference in value from one tier to the next. If the $15,000 sponsor package looks too close to the $10,000 sponsor package, it becomes too easy to select the $10,000 option. Be sure there's clear logic to why a sponsor should step up from one level to the next.

Use a small set of packages

Just as events and marketing professionals are tackling the learning curve of virtual events, so are event salespeople. A smaller comprehensive number of sponsorship packages will make it easier for sponsors and salespeople to digest.

You should start out with no more than five sponsorship packages. As your sponsors and your sales team get more comfortable, you can slowly start to build up the number of your offerings.

For hybrid events, create packages that combine physical and online.

Hybrid offers you expanded inventory options for sponsorships because you can combine elements of the virtual event and the onsite event.

Many of our hybrid clients have news desks onsite where they broadcast their programming to their virtual audience and their onsite audience. The same programming that runs over the virtual program will run at their physical event through their mobile app, on conference monitors in the convention centers, or on hotel TV channels so both audiences can see the same programming.

In addition to the virtual event elements that are monetizable, hybrid event sponsors can have branding visibility on the news desk itself, in communications promoting the news desk, have one of their executives be an on-air host for an hour, and much more. I'll provide some examples in the next section.

SAMPLE VIRTUAL EVENT SPONSORSHIP PACKAGES

Let's put everything that we talked about earlier in this chapter into action. Here are some real-life examples that you can use to build out your tiered sponsorships.

The examples below begin with a platinum sponsorship that will contain the most benefits and can be priced the highest. As we get down to gold, silver, etc., you'll see that the benefits and value reduce so you can price these lower.

Platinum Sponsorship

Exhibit Booth

- Custom-built exhibit booth with the following features:
  - Include welcome/product/services videos
  - Add product and sales materials to share with attendees visiting your booth
  - One-on-one chat capabilities to create engagement for your booth visitors

Branding and Visibility

- One display ad rotating in the lobby, lounge, and exhibit hall
- Logo recognition in the theatre
- Ability to have a single, rotating banner display ad each day that will be visible for up to 15 minutes before the beginning of each webcast content block; you have two content blocks per day

- One marquee message directing attendees to your booth in the exhibit hall per day

- Sponsorship logo recognition on all attendee emails

- One pop-up announcement message directing attendees to your booth per day

Gamification

- Create a company-specific badge; attendees must visit your booth and accomplish certain actions in order to earn it (can also host drawing for those who earned badge)

- Ability to draft one thought leadership trivia question that includes promotional messaging: "To find out more visit us in the exhibit hall"

Content

- 30-to-45-minute speaking opportunity

  - Two polling questions

  - Ability to have one to three links or handouts available during your session

  - Create a three-to-five-question survey that will come up at the end of your presentation

Post-Event Data

- Full list of all participants that visited your booth and downloaded assets and record of all booth chats

- Full list of all participants that attend your speaking session, all survey and polling responses, and record of all chats and Q&A

Gold Sponsorship

Exhibit Booth

- Custom-built exhibit booth with the following features:
  – Include welcome/product/services videos

- Add product and sales materials to share with attendees visiting your booth
- One-on-one chat capabilities to create engagement for your booth visitors

Branding and Visibility

- One display ad rotating in the lounge and exhibit hall
- Ability to have a single, rotating banner display ad each day that will be visible for up to 15 minutes before the beginning of each webcast content block; two content blocks per day
- One marquee message directing attendees to your booth in the exhibit hall per day
- Sponsorship logo recognition on all attendee emails

Gamification

- Ability to draft one thought leadership trivia question that includes promotional messaging: "To find out more visit us in the exhibit hall"

Content

- 15-to-30-minute speaking opportunity
  - Two polling questions
  - Ability to have one to three links or handouts available during your session
  - Create three-to-five-question survey that will come up at the end of your presentation

Post-Event Data

- Full list of all participants that visited your booth and downloaded assets and record of all booth chats
- Full list of all participants that attend your speaking session, all survey and polling responses, and record of all chats and Q&A.

Silver Sponsorship

Exhibit Booth

- Custom-built exhibit booth with the following features:
  - Include welcome/product/services videos
  - Add product and sales materials to share with attendees visiting your booth
  - One-on-one chat capabilities to create engagement for your booth visitors

Branding and Visibility

- One display ad rotating on the main page of the exhibit hall
- Ability to have a single, rotating display banner ad each day that will be visible for up to 15 minutes before the beginning of each webcast content block; two content blocks per day; runs on either day 1 or day 2
- Sponsorship logo recognition on all attendee emails

Gamification

- Ability to draft one thought leadership trivia question that includes promotional messaging: "To find out more visit us in the exhibit hall"

Post-Event Data

- Full list of all participants that visited your booth and downloaded assets and record of all booth chats

Bronze Sponsorship

Exhibit Booth

- Custom-built exhibit booth with the following features:
  - Include welcome/product/services videos
  - Add product and sales materials to share with attendees visiting your booth

    – One-on-one chat capabilities to create engagement for your booth visitors

Branding and Visibility

- Ability to have a single, rotating banner display ad each day that will be visible for up to 15 minutes before the beginning of each webcast content block; two content blocks per day; runs on either day 1 or day 2

Post-Event Data

- Full list of all participants that visited your booth and downloaded assets and record of all booth chats

SAMPLE HYBRID EVENT SPONSORSHIP PACKAGE

We've talked about hybrid events quite a bit and those, like virtual events, can be monetized. The difference is that you can expand the sponsorship package benefits by combining virtual event elements like I showed you above with live event programming elements to create new hybrid event sponsorship packages. Below is an example of a hybrid sponsorship package that is at that higher price point.

Dominance Sponsorship – Client Interview and Panel

Interview

- Exclusive interview at the news desk or at your booth location with program host featuring an executive from your organization (3–5 minutes)

- Representatives from your organization will be part of a three-to-four-person on-air panel with program host (5–7 minutes)

- On-air recognition as a sponsor

- Segments will be aired one time on one of the live broadcast days

Social Media Promotion

- Scheduled social media posts the week of the conference (1 tweet, 1 Facebook, 1 LinkedIn)
- A 15-to-30-second video clip will be pushed out to social channels during your live interview

Onsite Booth

- Two meeting pods
- 10'×10' space with seating for four
- Three full conference badges and eight exhibitor/client badges

Learning lounge recognition

- Electronic messaging billboards/entrance units promoting the learning lounge throughout the convention center
- Tuesday keynote session walk-in slides promoting learning lounge
- Signage promoting the learning lounge throughout the convention center
- Placement for company collateral in main area of the learning lounge

Virtual Exhibit Booth

- Custom-built exhibit booth with the following features:
  - Include welcome/product/services videos
  - Add product and sales materials to share with attendees visiting your booth
  - One-on-one chat capabilities to create engagement for your booth visitors

Advertising

- Your 30-second commercial will air twice per day within broadcast

- Your 15-second pre-roll will be included as part of the programming running on conference hotel TV channels

- Exclusive ownership of pre-roll advertising slot on company website; flight would last approx. 8 to 10 weeks.

Onsite Branding

- Your SME/executive will give opening and closing remarks each day of live programming (one to three minutes for each remark)

- Organization name and logo to appear on all news desk signage and news desk and key marketing promotions

As you can see there are a number of creative and different ways to monetize your event and make sponsorships available to customers at all price points. These are simply suggestions; you should try to think out of the box because nobody knows your industry better than you do. In the next chapter we'll look at how to market your virtual event.

CHAPTER **10**

Marketing Your Virtual Event

Now that you've selected a platform, finalized your content, and built your sponsorships, you need to develop a marketing strategy to differentiate your event in the marketplace and drive attendance.

Marketing a virtual event isn't so different than marketing a physical event. You're going to be using similar or almost identical marketing channels. The biggest differentiator that I see is that within your messaging you're going to have to make sure people understand and are comfortable with a virtual environment.

In this chapter, we'll talk about what your marketing timeline should look like, developing your message and the steps you should be taking to market pre-event, during the event, and post-event.

FIRST THINGS FIRST: ANSWERING KEY QUESTIONS AND ESTABLISHING KEY GOALS

Before you dive into your strategy, it's important to establish some key goals and have answers to questions that will have an impact on how you develop your plan.

- **What will success look like?** Is it number of registrants, qualified leads, etc.? The answer to this question is going to affect how you market. If success is getting as many registrants as possible, then you should open your marketing efforts to as wide an audience as you can. If a successful event means that you get a certain number of qualified leads, then you are going to spend more time on your audience segmentation strategy so you're sure to reach the right people.

- **What are your goals/objectives?** Are you looking to expand awareness across new audiences, create new revenue streams, reach a certain segment of your audience? These goals will again affect what marketing efforts you focus on. If your goal is to expand awareness, you'll need to consider if that means marketing to a segment of your audience you have never marketed events to before. You could also enter into marketing agreements with partners who will market to their audiences on your behalf. If you want to create new revenue streams, then you'll need to either focus more on your messaging to attendees so they're comfortable with the attendee registration fee for your virtual event or create a more robust sponsorship marketing plan that includes concise messaging for sponsors, so they see the value in purchasing your sponsorship packages.

- **What value are you providing?** When developing your messaging, make sure all your audiences see the value in attending. For sponsors that could be that they receive more attendee data than at a physical event, and for attendees it could be that they can earn educational credits or access sessions on-demand for six months after the event.

- **Is your marketing budget finalized?** Finalize all the marketing channels you will be using that require marketing dollars.

- **Do you have a content strategy?** Your content strategy is going to support your goals and success. Basically, it's the "why" behind building your content. What is this content going to solve and who is it going to reach? You need to answer these questions as they relate to each of your audience segments and channels, so you have an organized plan and aren't building content reactively.

MARKETING TIMELINE

Because the event is virtual and does not require your attendees to travel or be out of the office, your marketing timeline can be a bit more condensed. You should start marketing your event at least two to three months prior to your event date to reach your registration goal.

Our benchmark report found that over half of people who attended live, 58% to be exact, registered more than a week from the event date (Figure 10.1). Only 22% of those who registered two to seven days prior to the event date attended live and our live attendance numbers really drop for people that registered the day before or the day of.

That tells us that when attendees register so close to the event date, they don't really allocate the time on their calendars to tune in. Those that register earlier in the marketing cycle make the time to be present.

ESTABLISHING YOUR TARGET AUDIENCE

A target audience for a virtual event is the group of individuals that have similar needs and characteristics that a company can best serve with its product or service.

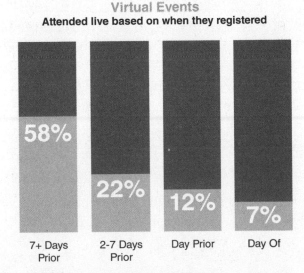

Figure 10.1   Those who attended live based on when they registered.

Answering these questions will help you to better understand your target audience:

- Who will be using this product or service and why?
- What industry are you targeting?
- What management level are you targeting?
- What business specialty are you targeting?
- What career level is your audience at?
- What makes the audience tick?
- What are their buying behaviors?
- Where do they go for information?
- How do they prefer to receive information?
- Why will they tune in?
- What content types do they prefer?
- What channels are they on?

BUILDING A STRONG MESSAGE

Your message is the foundation of your marketing plan and communicates the details, benefits, and value of your event.

- Tell your audience how you will solve their business problem or provide knowledge they want or that will help them achieve an organizational or personal goal.
- Segment your audience so that you can personalize your message by what is important to each group.
- Explain how you're different and better than your competitors.
- Clearly state the call to action. What do you want your audience to do when they are finished reading?

Tips to Building a Strong Message

- *Concise* – State your point first, then support it.

- *Highlight Value* – Define and address the benefits/value of your content.

- *Relevant* – Balance what you need to communicate with what your audience needs to know.

- *Compelling* – Your message should stimulate action.

- *Memorable* – Use copy that is easy to recall and repeat; avoid run-on sentences, less is more.

- *Simple* – Easy-to-understand language; avoid jargon and acronyms. Some of your readers might be new to the industry. Put the acronym in parentheses upon the first reference [e.g. American Medical Association (AMA)].

- *One-to-One* – Always strive to speak to one person, not "all of you."

- *Do It in Style* – Stay professional and focused but let your personality show.

- *Details Count* – Make sure to fix any typos or grammatical errors; they can taint the validity of your message.

- *Timing Is Everything* – Make sure you schedule multiple communications and give your audience time to act.

BUILDING A MESSAGING FRAMEWORK

Your messaging framework is going to have six basic steps. You can't include all these points in every message you write but you should have them established so you are delivering a consistent message in everything you write. For example, email copy may include all six points, but social media posts may focus on only one or two steps throughout your entire campaign.

1. *Capture Their Attention with a Strong Headline or Intro Line* – This can either be a strong email subject line, first sentence of your blog, or display ad copy.

2. *Identify Pain Points, Needs, or Wants* – This tells your audience what industry issue or challenge your content will solve, what new ideas or perspectives you can provide, or what new findings you can share.

3. *Provide a Brief Description of Your Event and What They Will Learn/Experience* – This answers the "What's in it for me?" question your audiences have. Why should they attend, register, and click when you ask them to?

4. *Describe the Benefit/Value to the Customer* – This is different than "What's in it for me?"; this point is more experiential. For virtual events this is where you include values like live speaker Q&A, real-time chat, and view live sessions you missed on-demand.

5. *Give Your Message Credibility* – Provide statistics, testimonials, or case studies whenever possible.

6. *State the Call to Action* – What do you want them to do: click here, register, sign up, etc.

Below I've laid out an example using ABC concert.

ABC Concert Example
Capture Their Attention with a Strong Headline

- ABC Concert is coming back to Greenview Park September 15–17, 2020

Identify Pain Points, Needs, or Wants

- The first wave of ABC Concert lineup will be announced April 19, 2020, early-bird tickets on sale now

- The second wave of lineups will be announced June 1 with full day-to-day schedule, layaway tickets available

Provide a Brief Description of Your Event and What They Will Learn/Experience

- ABC Concert is a multiday music festival specializing in punk, rock, alternative, metal, and hip-hop. ABC Concert was founded in 2000 in Chicago. In addition to live music, you will enjoy carnival rides, amazing food vendors, roving magicians, and more.

Describe the Benefit/Value to the Customer

- Live music, outside venue, and other entertainment
- Located in major city
- Hotel accommodations
- Multiple ticket tiers, kid friendly
- Updates on album releases, concerts, and band videos

Give Your Message Credibility

- "Best concert lineup in the Midwest"

State the Call to Action

- Buy Tickets Now; this discount price is only available for one more week.

Driving Audiences Pre-Event

Before the event, your objective is to maximize registrations from your target audience. Let your audience know the date and time, the featured presenters, and what's in it for them.

The first place prospects are going to go to learn about your event is to your event website, so this element of your plan must be up and active before any promotions can start. Your event website will be the first place prospective attendees will go to get more information and most of your marketing channels will take people here as well.

Feature the event's agenda, abstract, and speaker list. Include social icons that encourage visitors to share the event with their followers. The job of your website is to provide enough information to entice the visitor to register so it is imperative to have a live registration page when you launch your website. You don't ever want to have a message like "check back for registration information." Once you have an engaged prospect you don't want to put the responsibility on them to come back to your site when registration is open.

Your event website will be part of your overall company website so you will want to prominently feature the event on your company homepage by including it in a hero image or display ad. Also consider placing a fixed promotion above your site's main navigation using a tool such as Hello Bar.

Once your registration page is live you are going to want to integrate it into your Marketing Automation and CRM system, if appropriate, to ensure all your data is in one place for better segmentation, scoring, qualification, and sales follow-up.

Segmenting Your Audience

Segmenting your audiences to personalize your marketing messages in emails, website properties, and other marketing materials is the key to getting your prospects to pay attention. Using virtual event data and marketing automation you can elevate the impact of your message to your target audiences.

There are several ways for you to segment your audiences but don't go too granular because remember you're going to have to customize messaging in your channels for each segment.

Some ways to segment include:

- Those who attended your event last year
- Those who registered last year but didn't attend

- Those that have attended one or more webcast but not an event

- By specific management level or area of expertise

Marketing Channel Options

Your marketing channels are the vehicles you'll use to reach your audience. You'll want to have multiple channels as part of your plan so you can reach a broad audience and so your audience will see your message multiple times, which drives a higher probability of them taking the action you want, which is to register.

Prospect Emails

I've seen that email is the number-one driver of pre-event registrations. For virtual events, this is a good cadence to follow:

- Start sending messages to segmented audiences three months before the event

- During months two and three, email every two weeks

- Four weeks out from the event date you can send with this frequency:

  - Two weeks before the event

  - One week before the event

  - One day before the event

  - 15 minutes before the event

Test different subject lines and times of day to identify the best open, click-through, and registration rates. With this information you can adjust the content you include in your subject lines and the times of day you send emails to certain segments for maximum results.

Attendees' Emails

As I noted, your event registrants may register up to two months before the event date. Just because they registered doesn't mean they're going to actually attend.

Many times, I've seen clients send the "thank-you for registering" email and then have no contact with registrants and expect them to just show up.

You need to keep in contact with registrants and maintain that excitement through attendee nurturing email communications. These emails serve two purposes, to keep the event top of mind but to also put a focus on event speakers, topics, and exhibitors to sustain that excitement and motivate those registrants to convert to attendees.

Social Media

Schedule multiple posts across your active social channels (e.g. Twitter, LinkedIn, Facebook, Instagram). In order to achieve the best results, use your social channels that have already been established and have a strong following. Don't try to launch and activate a new social channel during your event campaign. That's an exercise that needs its own campaign.

Define a hashtag for your event and include it in all social media posts so that users can see all posts associated with your event through a hashtag search. Include images or video in your posts to grab user attention faster and more effectively. Also consider promoting the event in relevant LinkedIn Groups.

You should post one or two times per week beginning three months out from your event date and then post weekly or bi-weekly on all your channels one month out from the event date.

Blog and Vlog Posts

Write blog posts or create video blogs (vlogs) to promote the event. Make sure that all the content you feature is focused on the event. You can interview speakers and highlight exhibitors. You can also talk about the features and functionality of your virtual event and hype the benefits of going virtual.

Press Release

A press release will not only target industry journalists but also bloggers and other writers. Send out a press release to announce the virtual event and make sure to mention key sessions and speakers. Include the event registration link in the press release.

Search Engine Marketing (SEM), Also Known as Paid Search

Search engine marketing is a form of internet marketing that promotes websites by increasing their visibility in search engine results primarily through paid advertising.

Consider allocating a portion of your budget to pay-per-click (PPC) advertising. Your PPC ads on Google and Bing will drive targeted visitors to your event's landing page.

Paid Media/Industry Partnerships

Team up with associations or partners with a membership base that fits your audience profile. Leverage digital programs such as sponsored newsletters, display ads, and email blasts to get in front of them.

Engage and Activate Influencers

Industry influencers can promote your virtual event and encourage their followers to register and attend. Start first with your event's speakers. Arm speakers with social media posts that they can share with their followers. Record short videos with speakers and upload the videos natively to your Twitter, Facebook, LinkedIn, etc., profiles and make sure to tag your speaker.

Measure, Evaluate, and Adapt

As your campaign gets underway, be sure to always take a step back to see how your campaign is performing and evaluate what adjustments you can make based on the channel data you have. Here are a few ways you can do that:

- Implement tracking links for all channels, sponsors, speakers, etc., so you know where your registrants are coming from. Maintain a master list of your tracking links so you can keep track of all your sources.

- Use Google Analytics, Facebook Insights, AdWords dashboards, and other reporting tools to see which virtual event promotions are working well. Optimize future promotions based on these findings.

- Check your registration list to see what audience you are not reaching. Is there a channel you aren't yet leveraging?

- Encourage registrants to share the event with their networks. Post a message such as "I've registered for VIRTUAL EVENT LIVE, happening on June 29th. Won't you join me?"

- Share results and recommendations with executive sponsors and stakeholders. If appropriate, ask them for feedback and suggestions.

Day-of-Event Promotion

It's the day of your event, and it's still not too late to drive attendance to your event not only from those that registered but also from prospects.

The channels that I've found that work best to drive "day of" attendees are email, social media, and word of mouth.

Email

Reach out to your two main segments on the day of the event. These are some high-level email topics you can use:

Registrants

- Reminder email the day of
  - Don't miss your event starting today

- Reminder email 15 minutes before
  - Shut down now; don't be late

- 10 minutes into the event email those not in the event
  - This is the session you're missing

Prospects

- Reminder email the day of
  - Still time to attend

- Reminder email 5 to 10 minutes before
  - Shut down now; still time to attend
- 10 minutes into the event email those not in the event
  - This is the session you're missing

Social Media

Peak your audiences' interest and tap into their "fear of missing out." These are some ways you can message on social while your event is going on:

Twitter

- Live tweeting throughout the event
- Ask speakers to tweet the day of the presentation before they go on
- Sponsors can tweet about who is online and what they are offering at their booth

Facebook

- Short post featuring your event's welcome video
- Post updates leading up to sessions
  - What you will learn, speaker bio, etc.
- Ask speakers and sponsors to post

LinkedIn

- Frequency is less than Facebook and Twitter. Post not only to your LI but also to all applicable groups
- Ask speakers and sponsors to make a content-based post the day of presentation and provide link to event. You could use teaser slides of presentations as part of your post.

Word of Mouth

All client-facing employees should contact key prospects who are not in the event yet. Ask employees to log into environment the first 5 to 10 minutes to see who is there and reach out to customers to remind them of the event and give them a nudge to attend.

Keeping Your Attendees Engaged

After those final efforts to get attendees, you are going to have a good-sized audience attending your virtual event, which means increased pressure to keep them engaged.

Here's how to create an interactive experience so your audience becomes an active participant instead of a passive listener:

- Upload content and highlights in real-time. Publish key take-aways to social media, email, and blog posts throughout the event to create buzz.

- Continuously tap into attendee recognition. Leverage badging and gamification elements for attendee engagement and participation. Leaderboards can be used as a real-time recognition vehicle for active participants in the event.

- Use in-event lounges. In-event chats can be used to easily share content without leaving the experience. For example, announce details of the latest prize or highlight the person atop the leaderboard.

- Dedicate a social media moderator on your team. Having an individual watching over chatter and making timely updates can keep the audience engaged.

Having a Strategy for Marketing Your Event After It's On-Demand

At the conclusion of the live virtual event, many event planners think that most of the work is done. The savvy event planners, however, realize the power and potential of the on-demand period. It's an opportunity to keep your audience engaged and continue to drive toward your goals (e.g. number of registrations, getting that important target audience to view your content).

Post-Event Follow-Up

After the live virtual event, leverage the on-demand period to engage registrants who couldn't attend live and stay engaged with people who attended the live event.

Review your analytics to learn how viewers engaged with your event, sponsors, fellow attendees, and sessions. Invite users to take an online survey to share their input about the event.

Follow up with attendees who had heavy participation, earned badges, or won prizes and get their feedback or conduct longer interviews with them.

Email Campaigns

Deploy an email campaign to remind people of the on-demand access. Invite them into the environment to view presentations on-demand. This is the communication structure that I've found to be most effective:

Registrants

- Thank-you-for-attending email
  - Promote on-demand, ask for referrals
  - Include any promised materials
- Short survey of the event

Registrants Who Did Not Attend

- Promote on-demand; ask to refer to employees and colleagues
- Provide a suggestion for another event or piece of content relevant to an event topic

Prospects

- "Sorry we missed you" email
  - Promote on-demand
- Provide suggestion for another event or piece of content relevant to an event topic

Repurpose Content or Follow Up on Presentations

Just because your event is over doesn't mean that the content is stale. It can be repurposed, or elements like case studies or research reports that were launched at your event can become mini–content campaigns in themselves. You can also identify the most popular sessions and rerun them live or have a secondary presentation that addresses the questions that couldn't be answered in the prior presentation.

Below are some ways you can generate new content assets from your virtual event content:

- Snackable videos or vlogs
- Blog articles
- Infographics
- Webinar series
- Podcasts
  - Create or add new content into the virtual environment and inform participants via email blasts and social media.

Checklist for Success

Follow this checklist to create an effective post–virtual event strategy.

1. **Thank your audience for attending.**

    Let your attendees know you appreciate them. Let them know what's coming next, such as future events or webinars.

2. **Send out feedback surveys.**

    Survey your audience, both quantitatively and qualitatively. Ask for numeric ratings on key elements of the virtual event and ask them to share their comments. Ask what topics they'd like to see covered in future events. This data will be helpful as you build your next event so that you can include more of the content and interactions attendees liked and tweak the parts of the event that weren't as popular.

3. **Reemphasize your virtual event several times, several ways.**

    Remind the audience about on-demand access and send periodic reminders highlighting popular sessions.

4. **Build a relationship with your audience.**

Send personalized messages to thank people who asked questions or shared insights. Are there any influencers or advocates to engage with for your next virtual event? Connect with them on LinkedIn and stay in touch.

I've emphasized how important virtual event data is throughout this book. The next chapter jumps into detail on the data you can pull and the value it provides you, your exhibitors, and your sponsors.

CHAPTER 11

The Power of Virtual Event Data

I think one of the most game-changing benefits that a virtual event can offer you is the amount of data that we can provide about attendee activity. This data benefits you, as the event organizer, because it tells you what sessions were the most popular and well attended, who was there, and how long they stayed. For sponsors and exhibitors, data can tell you who visited your booth or clicked on your ad and what else that individual person did while they were engaging with you. And finally, for your marketers, this rich data can help them to build detailed a lead scoring model.

In this chapter I'll go through in detail what reports you can get from a virtual event and take you through how you can use that data to build your lead scoring model.

TAKING ADVANTAGE OF VIRTUAL EVENT DATA

Let me explain to you exactly why data is such a game changer for virtual events. At a physical event you may get the list of people who registered and those who attended. There will be badge scanners that capture those people who walked into a session room but how long did they stay, did they ask a question? Badge scanners will also tell you who was in your booth, but did they talk to anyone, were they there to grab a giveaway, and then did they leave?

Virtual event data can give you a series of reports to answer these questions and so much more. Here's the breakdown of what you can expect.

Programming Key Data Points

As you know by now, all your sessions are packaged as webcasts of different lengths. You will be able to collect the following reports for each of your webcasts.

Your virtual event provider should build a high-level dashboard for you that will include the following items:

- The current status of the webcast (Live, On-Demand, Starts In...)

- Total Registrants, Total Attended (Live and On-Demand), Live Conversation Rate, and Average View Time

- Interactivity with Polling Questions, Q&A, Documents Accessed (Handouts), and Group Chat Lines

- Viewers by Browser

- Viewers by OS

Individual Reports

Each of the reports I've listed below track all the individual actions taken throughout the event that you can get data on:

- *Registration* – Includes registered versus attended, registration page hits, number of registrants for each day, and affiliate data tracking complete with conversion rates.

- *Live Attendance Trends* – Minute-by-minute breakdown of attendance during live run of the webcast. This report will highlight peak number of viewers, unique live viewers, when viewers joined and left the webcast, providing insight into audience interest in the content.

- *On-Demand Attendance Trends* – Day-by-day breakdown of attendance during the on-demand period including the number of unique viewers by the most active day.

- *Question and Answers* – Summary of question status (asked, answered, ignored, approved, untouched) and trend tracking to determine volume of questions during live run of the webcast. Provide this report to speakers after the live broadcast to review activity and follow up with users.

- *Group Chat* – Trend tracking to determine volume of chat activity during live broadcast of the webcast. A full transcript of all chat activity can be reviewed and exported.

- *Polling Questions* – Summary of all polls pushed during the webcast and the number of respondents during the webcast and unique viewers.

- *Surveys* – Includes number of responses to each question and a breakdown of the responses. This also measures the number of users who viewed the question but elected not to answer.

- *Handouts* – Total document views and unique viewers.

- *"Invite a Friend" Activity* – Includes all "Invite a Friend" usage, and conversion rates to registrations.

- *Messaging* – Complete tracking of all messaging activity, such as when the email was sent, whether it was opened, bounced, unopened, and additional details on potential reasons for the bounced emails.

- *Technical Data* – Summary of users by platform and browser to evaluate the devices (e.g. desktop, mobile) and other information on how participants engaged with the webcast.

- *Speaker Activity* – A comprehensive log of all presenter actions such as starting the webcast, transitioning slides, and pushing polls to the audience.

- *Benchmarks* – Compare one webcast to another. Allowing the ability to compare registration versus attended conversion, live to on-demand conversion, average view time, average webcast duration, and polling responses.

- *Quality of Experience (QoE) Report* – Summary of users based on the quality of their viewing experience. The report shows viewer activity for each person who was on the webcast. If that user had issues, you will be able to see errors, buffering, quality level changes, and more summed with each viewer update, which is collected every 10 seconds.

All this information will enable you to score leads, see what topics and sessions resonated the most, which handouts were most downloaded, and so much more. This reporting also provides more value to your sponsors and is a strong argument you can use to justify the value you are providing to them through their sponsorship and exhibit opportunity. Lastly, you will be able to make data-driven decisions on how you update your event for next time.

MANAGING AND SCORING VIRTUAL EVENT LEADS

I believe that interaction has replaced consumption. The use of real-time virtual event engagement tools (e.g. interactive polls, Q&A, group chat) creates an experience that engages prospects.

The average virtual event is ripe with data collection opportunities to enhance brand awareness, nurture leads, and drive sales. Integrating your marketing automation platform (MAP) and your Customer Relationship Management (CRM) system with your online event will provide more data with less effort, easing the strain of parsing through bulk lists and spending exorbitant amounts of time chasing uninterested leads.

To date, web analytics (i.e. for your corporate website) have focused on static measures, such as page views, bounce rate, time on site, and pages per session.

With virtual events, we've again moved up the value chain. Now, we can analyze answers to polling questions, percent of program viewed, questions submitted to the presenter, and chat messages contributed to the conversation.

With web analytics, you decipher what they consumed.

With a virtual events platform, you know what participants consumed, but – more importantly – you also know what they said and how they feel (Figure 11.1).

But remember, with event data, just because you can collect it doesn't necessarily mean it will all be useful. The key to getting the most out of your online event and MAP integration is to match your goals with the appropriate event metrics and KPIs (see Figure 11.2).

Lead Management

Virtual events and webcasts are no longer only for "top of the funnel" leads; they're a great way to engage and rank suspects, prospects, and nurtured leads at different levels in your sales funnel. In fact, webcasts are a fantastic way to influence decision-makers as they make their final purchase choice.

Most virtual event platforms provide event hosts with access to a real-time dashboard that tracks all attendee activity. The tracking begins with event registration and progresses to sessions attended, documents downloaded, spaces visited, and more.

This activity data can enrich your attendee profiles, further qualify your prospects, and give you a better understanding of what your audience is interested in. In turn, it can create more personalized follow-up and nurturing.

From the increased level of interaction, think about the wealth of engagement data that will now be included in your CRM and MAP systems. By integrating key data into your marketing automation and CRM platforms you will be able to establish proper lead scoring and follow-up strategies to qualify leads and move them down the funnel (as shown in Figure 11.3).

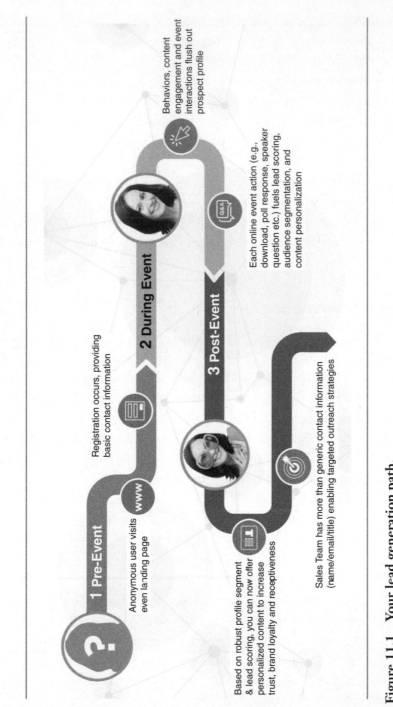

1 Pre-Event

Anonymous user visits even landing page

Registration occurs, providing basic contact information

2 During Event

Behaviors, content engagement and event interactions flush out prospect profile

3 Post-Event

Each online event action (e.g., download, poll response, speaker question etc.) fuels lead scoring, audience segmentation, and content personalization

Based on robust profile segment & lead scoring, you can now offer personalized content to increase trust, brand loyalty and receptiveness

Sales Team has more than generic contact information (name/email/title) enabling targeted outreach strategies

Figure 11.1 Your lead generation path.

	Registration & Attendance	Lead Generation	Brand Awareness	Content Engagement
Total # of Attendees	●		●	
% Increase YOY	●	●	●	
Average # Sessions Attended	●			
Registration to Attendee Conversion %	●	●		
Affiliate Tracking	●	●	●	
Sponsor Booth Visits	●	●		
Sessions Attended		●		
Average Session Duration		●	●	●
Chat/Q&A Participation		●		●
Polling Responses		●		●
Downloaded Materials		●		●
Badges Earned				●
Social Media Posts/Shares				●
Display Advertising Clicks		●	●	●
Survey Results		●		●

Figure 11.2   Matching the virtual event data points to your KPIs.

OTHER LEAD MANAGEMENT STEPS YOU CAN TAKE:

- Send qualified leads to sales via integration between your virtual event platform and your CRM system (e.g. prioritize the warm leads that clicked on a CTA in the event asking to speak with sales).

- Review chat transcripts for clues on prospects' sales readiness. For example, questions about product features and pricing may indicate that prospects are actively researching for a product purchase.

Lead Nurturing

Once you get all your leads in from your event you can't treat them all the same way. Some are at the purchase stage while others are higher in the sales funnel. By developing a lead nurturing strategy, you can push those leads through the funnel.

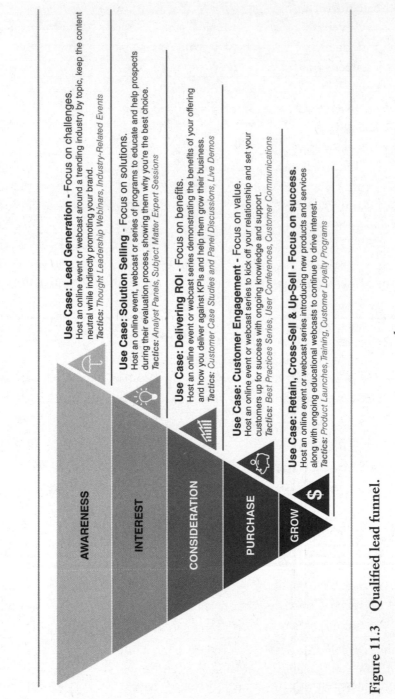

Use Case: Lead Generation - Focus on challenges.
Host an online event or webcast around a trending industry by topic, keep the content neutral while indirectly promoting your brand.
Tactics: Thought Leadership Webinars, Industry-Related Events

Use Case: Solution Selling - Focus on solutions.
Host an online event, webcast or series of programs to educate and help prospects during their evaluation process, showing them why you're the best choice.
Tactics: Analyst Panels, Subject Matter Expert Sessions

Use Case: Delivering ROI - Focus on benefits.
Host an online event or webcast series demonstrating the benefits of your offering and how you deliver against KPIs and help them grow their business.
Tactics: Customer Case Studies and Panel Discussions, Live Demos

Use Case: Customer Engagement - Focus on value.
Host an online event or webcast series to kick off your relationship and set your customers up for success with ongoing knowledge and support.
Tactics: Best Practices Series, User Conferences, Customer Communications

Use Case: Retain, Cross-Sell & Up-Sell - Focus on success.
Host an online event or webcast series introducing new products and services along with ongoing educational webcasts to continue to drive interest.
Tactics: Product Launches, Training, Customer Loyalty Programs

AWARENESS

INTEREST

CONSIDERATION

PURCHASE

GROW

$

Figure 11.3 Qualified lead funnel.

Lead nurturing is the process of developing relationships with buyers at every stage of the sales funnel. The engagement and behavioral data you've gathered from your event will be used to assess the needs of prospects and provide the information and answers they need.

A good MAP can help you to develop your lead nurture campaign. Marketing automation platforms exist to process, analyze, and respond to all these data sets we've been talking about.

Think of marketing automation like a Roomba. Out of the box, it's a vacuum cleaning robot. Without setting up any initial parameters and providing opportunities for learned intelligence, it will simply bash around your house blindly until it eventually figures things out.

When used properly, your little Roomba can scale your house-keeping efforts by alleviating the traditional process of vacuuming, enabling you to work smarter, not harder.

Marketing automation, when configured properly with your online events, will:

- Allow you to map each phase of the attendee event experience while propagating profile data to amplify your marketing efforts and support your event KPIs.

- Equip your sales team with an arsenal of rich data empowering them to confidently hone in on the hottest prospects for increased revenue.

- Provide rich prospect data to nurture leads with personalized content and inform targeted outreach strategies.

Lead nurture campaigns that leverage emails sent out on a specific cadence can be enhanced with virtual event attendee data. Attendees can receive nurture content that relates directly to the content they consumed at the event. After creating multiple emails with targeted content to fit your specific use case, you can set the cadence of your emails. You can create multiple lists of attendees that fit specific personas, levels of qualification, or product interest. The more specific you make your nurture emails, the better the results.

Lead Quality

Online events and lead generation efforts often succumb to the same philosophy that quantity somehow trumps quality (e.g., "more attendees will equal more opportunities to convert leads into prospects"). In theory, that would only be true if you had unlimited time and resources to chase lukewarm to cold leads.

For example, if you are planning a lead generation event targeting developers in the startup community, would you rather have a random mix of 20,000 event planners, stay-at-home moms, and retired principals attend your event, or 10,000 actual programmers/developers in the startup community?

Lead Scoring

Armed with this additional data, you're now able to segment your prospects effectively. You can configure lead-scoring formulas in your marketing automation system that map to interaction points within the event and webcasts (e.g. time viewed, questions asked, and chat messages submitted).

Data from physical events typically can only provide registered versus attended lists or data on who entered a session room.

You can score leads based on whether they registered or attended. In addition, you can increase their score based on how engaged they were in the webcast and event.

Lead scoring can be a very useful marketing automation tool for properly qualifying leads who are marketing qualified and sales qualified. Robust scoring models can pinpoint the sweet spot for when a lead is ready to be contacted by sales. By pairing lead scoring with your virtual event data, you can gain valuable insight into your leads and their position in the sales cycle.

Once you outline the information that would be most valuable to your use case as a trigger for someone who is "qualified," you can set up a specific campaign that listens and looks for these triggers to complete some action. Each organization will differ, but it is common practice to send an email to the sales representative once one of their assigned prospects becomes qualified based on the rules and triggers outlined from the virtual event.

In this alert email, you can include basic information about the lead and use tokens to pull in the specific triggers from the virtual event that designated them to become qualified. Using data collected from virtual events in lead-scoring programs enhances your marketing qualification strategy immensely because this behavioral information is collected behind the scenes.

In a virtual event, leads can create their own personalized experience without being pursued by a salesperson; as a result, their activity is completely authentic and can signal the proper time when sales should step in. Lead scoring allows the lead to signal where they fit in the sales cycle without them even knowing.

Figure 11.4 shows a sample of how you may break up your lead scoring for a virtual event. The way you score may change depending on your event, content, and needs.

Lead-Scoring Worksheet

Update and edit with your own models based on your event needs. Your lead score tiers and follow-up tactics can be edited to match your organization's sales model.

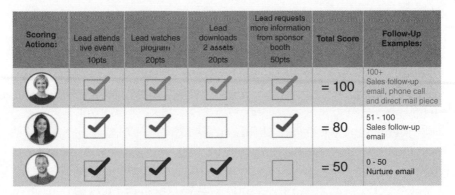

Scoring Actions:	Lead attends live event 10pts	Lead watches program 20pts	Lead downloads 2 assets 20pts	Lead requests more information from sponsor booth 50pts	Total Score	Follow-Up Examples:
	✓	✓	✓	✓	= 100	100+ Sales follow-up email, phone call and direct mail piece
	✓	✓		✓	= 80	51 - 100 Sales follow-up email
	✓	✓	✓		= 50	0 - 50 Nurture email

Figure 11.4   Your lead scoring report per individual.

Online Event Actions:	Score
Company Name (Target ABM Account)	40
Job Title (Includes Marketing)	20
Registers for Event	10
Attends Event	20
Views Session	30
Views All Sessions	65
Views On-Demand Recording	40
Answers Polling Question During Session	30
Responds to Survey	30
Downloads Asset	25
Visits sponsor booth	15
Requests More Information from Sponsor Booth	75
Custom Action (Interacted in Event)	
Custom Action (Total Time Spent in Event)	
Insert Your Own Actions!	

Lead Score	Follow-Up Tactic
200+ pts	Sales phone call, email, and special discount pricing on product for engagement
101–200 pts	Sales follows up with email and direct mail piece based on in-event actions
51–100 pts	Sales follows up with a personalized email about their visit
0–50 pts	Receives nurture emails until signaling they are ready to buy

Remember data is powerful and we only gave you some ways you can track the data from your event. I believe as a team you need to determine before the event how you will use the mountain of data that you will be able to attain from your event or series of events.

Conclusion: Virtual Events Are Here to Stay

Throughout the chapters of this book, my goal was to give you the tools you need to successfully make the shift from physical to virtual events. The COVID-19 pandemic has been a catalyst for change in the events industry – there is no going back to the way it was before. There will always be physical events, but now, finally, the world has seen the power of virtual events and how they can amplify physical events to educate, entertain, and successfully conduct business. The industry will continue to evolve, and the future is bright.

I'm not the only person who believes this, and I've asked a few people whom I really respect in this industry to share their opinions on why virtual events are here to stay.

The First Step Is the Hardest

Malcom Lotzof is one of the founders of INXPO and a good friend. He's one of the few people who has been in this space as long as I have. This is what he had to say:

> At some point, every industry will be disrupted by technology. It's just a matter of how and when it will happen. For the physical events industry, that time is now. Over the past few years, one of the most powerful advances to the internet has been the evolution of video. Today, the quality of managed video matches that of TV. When you integrate the power of broadcast TV into virtual events, they become TV-like experiences with the added benefit of live interaction between all participants. This development on its own has dramatically accelerated the adoption of virtual events.

The COVID-19 pandemic has all but eliminated physical events for an unknown period of time. But the need to move forward with hosted events continues, and many organizations have had to quickly adopt virtual events, and they've done it, almost entirely without missing a beat.

The results of virtual event adoption have been spectacular for many organizations. While physical events will come back because of their intimate, in-person networking capabilities, the numbers of participants at virtual events are far exceeding their physical counterparts because activity is far more trackable, and attendance is not affected by pandemic and other travel restrictions. Combine these advantages with the fact that virtual events can cost less than physical events and have a zero-carbon footprint. Their continued adoption and growth are a force of nature rather than a "nice to have" option.

For all of these reasons, I believe that when physical events do return they will and should be hybrid, with both physical and virtual components.

I told you Malcom was wise, and I am humbled that I get to call him a friend and partner.

IT'S ALL ABOUT COMMUNICATING

Scott Farb is an event producer whom I have known for over a decade, and he knows what he is talking about when it comes to events. He also has a really cool title, CEO and Chief Streaming Officer at StreamVPG in New York City, a virtual and physical event production company. Here's what he had to say about the future of virtual events:

Communication is the key to business; management communicating with employees, salespeople communicating with clients, and service people communicating with users. Live, in-person events and meetings were always the preference for these communication flows. We have learned over the past 20 years that getting the information out in a timely fashion was becoming more important, and webcasting became a great tool for quickly pushing that content out to global audiences. Now, with the ability to create a more immersive experience using virtual event tools to engage your audiences and extend your reach, people are realizing that they don't need to depend only on in-person events for networking or to deliver content to their audiences. With the virtual event tools we have today, and the ever-expanding functionality they provide, virtual events have become a critical part of your business and communications strategy. In-person events are not going away, but they are going to look a lot different and will need to include some element of online experience for audiences that can't or won't be able to attend in person.

WHEN VIRTUAL BECAME THE ONLY OPTION

Dan Rehal is the CEO of Vision2Voice Communications, a pharmaceutical marketing and event firm that has always been on the cutting edge of moving physical events into the world of virtual. So naturally, I wanted Dan to share his thoughts. He also shared a case study on behalf of one of his clients and their success evolving from in-person to virtual events:

> Prior to COVID-19, we sat at the strategy table with our client attempting to convince them to train their 600 clinical and scientific speakers using both virtual and live training sessions. We wanted to offer 600 busy scientists the option to gather in one location for an entire weekend of training, or have access to the same content from the comfort of their homes. We live in a fast-paced world – these speakers are doctors, and like everyone else, they are busy. As the world continues to evolve, we believe that virtual speaking and virtual speaker training are pivotal components of modern healthcare and medical

communications, and clients with speakers' bureaus must be ready to feature virtual as part of their communications strategies. In this particular case, however, our client told us repeatedly that they weren't ready and were unlikely to get approval in the very conservative world of biopharmaceuticals.

In an industry where federal guidance mandates rigorous training of contracted speakers in order for them to be part of a speaker's bureau, our client has always been very committed to live speaker training. In fact, they were so committed that they required all speakers to attend in person in order to remain in their bureau. If they didn't get their required training, they wouldn't be able to participate for the year, which is standard practice in biopharma.

Then everything changed. A massive snowstorm hit during the week of their scheduled in-person training, crippling travel. Not even company personnel would make it to the meeting destination in Florida. Due to the storm, more than 100 speakers couldn't attend live training. At the same time, the client had no infrastructure built or plans in place to conduct virtual training via the web.

They came to the Vision2Voice Communications team to provide a virtual solution. After reviewing their robust technical, legal, regulatory, and medical requirements, we created an action plan using our existing tools and implemented them to perfectly suit the client's needs.

First, we proposed a series of web events. The Vision2Voice client services and tech teams worked together in our Chicago command center to ensure high control over all of the program details.

Second, we needed hours to train the trainers. The faculty learned how to use the technology platform in advance, along with tips and tricks to effectively communicate on a virtual platform to maximize impact. Everyone was prepared to hit the ground running.

Third, we agreed on the value of interactivity. If attendees didn't respond to polling during an event, compliance didn't want them to be certified and they would have to attend an additional program. Having a proven method to track that attendees were interacting, learning, and committed to the new information was an important objective in order for the client to accept virtual training as a legitimate option to in-person training.

The results were astounding. Due to a defined partnership, commitment to excellence, our team-centered virtual approach, and our client's willingness to fully prepare their speakers, the participation rate was 99% – the first time the client had such a high percentage of the speakers bureau trained before the deadline. Their cost savings for virtual training was also significant compared to the cost of training the same number of speakers in person.

LIVE, VIRTUAL, AND HYBRID: SAME GAME, DIFFERENT TACTICS

Michael McCauley is president of Frictionless Solutions and someone with whom I had the privilege of working on some exciting events in the early days of virtual events almost 20 years ago. I asked Michael his thoughts on the future of virtual events:

Based on my experience helping many clients pivot from a live-only event strategy to one with both virtual and hybrid events, it helps to consider the game of football.

While the game is the same, you have different highly specialized "sides" to each tactic you are taking within the overall strategy to achieve a win: offense specializes in their area of expertise, defense has its own skill sets, and special teams fill the gap in transitions within the game.

As we help clients with their pivot strategies to augment, amplify, or replace live-only events, we ensure that while the game is the same, we need to focus on each tactic to drive the overall goal for winning: interactive and business specific attendee engagements.

What works in a live environment may not translate to a virtual or hybrid engagement, just as if you took your all-pro linebacker and put him in at quarterback!

Nothing beats experience as you look at options to leverage virtual and hybrid solutions whether it is the technology solution you need to support them or the support services to bring the same attention to detail as you would for your standalone live event.

Just as our clients developed a strategy supported by business objectives for live events, we strongly recommended they put the same discipline to their options, tactics, and technology choices for both virtual and hybrid events.

Two of the most important considerations are presenters and attendee experiences in a live environment, and it should not be assumed that both will be (or should be) the same in a virtual or hybrid event as they would be during in-person events.

We strongly advise clients to consider that what may work well in a live environment may not necessarily translate to virtual or hybrid events. In fact, through a strategic approach that includes robust, configurable, and user-friendly technology, a virtual and/or hybrid event may provide a better viewing and attendee experience with corresponding higher return on investment (ROI) than a live event.

Just like live events, it's important to start with the "who" of a virtual or hybrid event and consider the presenters and attendees who can best interact to accomplish the ultimate educational, business, or networking goals. Then consider what the focus of content will be for both the presenter and audience, and maximize the viewing experience using graphics, video, and other visual elements to reinforce that content. Finally, consider the best technology options to support your presenters, attendees, and content to make every element of your virtual or hybrid event as engaging as a live event.

It's important to remember that despite the use of so much technology with virtual and hybrid events, there are human resources who play a critical role in event success. No technology on its own can solve all of the challenges of virtual or hybrid events without the support of experienced and dedicated resources, and vice versa.

I can't thank Malcolm, Scott, Dan, and Mike enough for contributing to this book, and for their friendship through the years.

TECHNOLOGIES DRIVING THE FUTURE OF VIRTUAL EVENTS

So where are we going next? I believe the future of virtual events is fueled by innovation in technology and continued creativity. Augmented reality (AR), artificial intelligence (AI), virtual reality (VR), and technology that is not yet created will each shape the next generation of virtual events and will play a transformative role. You'll be able to be educated and entertained, and you'll be able to conduct business in immersive environments. Even more exciting is that you'll actually feel like you are at a physical venue and be able to experience people and products "in person" and in real time. You'll have the ability to have random encounters and interact with content that feels like it was designed just for you.

Let me explain how I see this working. Augmented reality combines the real and virtual worlds and integrates them within a virtual environment. It takes things one step further than integrating a live video feed into a virtual environment and introduces computer-generated senses like sound, sight, touch, and smell.

I have said for years that the only thing that a virtual event can't deliver to attendees is physical touch – the ability to shake hands, go for a walk, hold items – and the ability to smell and taste products. Think about how amazing it would be to go to a virtual conference and when you interact with an exhibitor's booth or a hands-on lab, you'd be able to virtually touch and use products. At a healthcare conference, for example, you could hold tools in your hands or see a demonstration of administered medicine as it enters a person's bloodstream. This technology exists; it just needs to be developed for the world of virtual events.

Virtual reality is a computer-generated artificial environment that you experience with sight and sound, and your specific actions can sometimes dictate what happens next. VR is most popular in the gaming industry, and you've probably seen people wearing virtual headsets and large virtual reality goggles on TV or in the movies. You might have even been part of a VR experience yourself.

Many agree VR is the next stage of virtual events. Imagine if attendees could simply put on their headsets and be transported to a virtual event where they felt like they were walking through a convention center, visiting exhibitor booths, shaking hands with delegates, or asking questions from their seat during the keynote session. At hybrid events, attendees could interact with each other in an in-person environment, then put on their goggles and interact with other attendees in the VR version of the event. This will be a game-changer for events, and the good news is that this technology is already here!

Artificial intelligence involves computers performing tasks that require human intelligence or decision-making skills. Think of speech recognition, where a computer creates a transcription of spoken words, and visual perception, like the app on your phone that uses the camera to read text and translate it to another language. An example of AI decision-making is the "you might also like" suggestions on Spotify after you download a certain song into your playlist.

What I like about this, and what I think is missing from a lot of events today, is the ability for the host technology to know what I am looking for and what I am interested in when I attend a virtual event.

Think about how great it would be if the event technology knew what sessions I would be interested in and who I might want to meet, based on what I did or who I talked to at the same event the year before. And what if content and experiences could be recommended to me based on what I downloaded or read on the event host's website, just like Amazon and Netflix make recommendations based on what I last watched or purchased. The ultimate AI-enabled virtual event experience for me would be when I logged into the platform and was greeted with, "Hello, Ben, and welcome. You may be interested in these sessions because you have done this or downloaded that…"

How we interact with each other in person and virtually is always changing, and technology is advancing at a faster rate than ever before. When it comes to events, there is no one-size-fits-all, out-of-the-box solution for everyone. But the communications technology in front of us – and just on the horizon – presents us with incredible opportunities to showcase our brands, connect global audiences, and "wow" our customers. The biggest mistake an organization can make is *not* to change, and to keep doing things one way because "that's the way it's always been done."

Change is unpredictable and it can feel uncomfortable, and as you transition to virtual and hybrid events, you'll likely be faced with some challenges. I encourage you to see them as opportunities and to embrace your new adventure. The future of events – and the value they can bring to your organization – is in your hands. If you put into practice some of the recommendations in this book, and think outside the box, I'm confident you'll be pleased with your results (and your audiences will be, too).

After reading this book, I hope you take away at least three things:

- My passion for digital and event technology within the communications industry. I've spent the better part of my professional career in an industry that depends and thrives on technology, and I firmly believe that there isn't an industry as innovative, entrepreneurial, and ready for disruption as the communications industry. In 2020 we're just scratching the surface of what we can do with AI, AR, and VR as enhancements to virtual events, and we've learned (perhaps by necessity) that business can not only pivot from in-person events to virtual and hybrid, they can reach new levels of success.

- Tools and know-how to help you transition to virtual events. Whether you're new to virtual events and wondering how to take the first step, or you're a seasoned pro looking to up-level your virtual events strategy, I hope you found the information in this book helpful. It's important to remember that this is a transition and not the flip of a switch. Like any venture with new technology, make sure the choices you make and the platforms you choose are the right ones for your business and the ones that will help you achieve your objectives.

- The confidence to champion virtual and hybrid events within your organization. You may find that your virtual events journey is met with hesitation and a lack of confidence from internal stakeholders. To an extent, this is understandable; new experiences often cause discomfort. Lead by example, be the go-to resource for virtual events within your organization, and bring others along for the adventure – PR, marketing, corporate communications, and even the C-suite. The best way for your organization to understand the untapped value of virtual events is to show them.

Thank you for beginning your journey with me and for reading this book. May your road ahead be an exciting one that's filled with adventure and great success.

ABOUT THE AUTHORS

Over the past twenty-five years, **Ben Chodor** has established himself as a global leader in the world of digital media and enterprise communications. He was Co-Founder and CEO of Happtique and Founder and CEO of Stream57, one of the first successful streaming/virtual event companies founded in early 2000, and led his companies through acquisitions. Ben was also Global Head of Streaming and Virtual Events at InterCall/West, which acquired his company, where he was a tireless driving force behind the company's innovative solutions. Ben is now President of Intrado DM, where he leads the organization in expanding its best-in-class solutions in public relations, investor relations, marketing, web hosting, media monitoring, and virtual and streaming events, with offices in 17 countries and over 1,200 dedicated professionals helping organizations deliver their mission-critical communications by running and managing virtual and streaming events for thousands of companies globally.

Ben is an enthusiastic, energetic leader with an incomparable passion for technology. He has spent his career pioneering online communications through interactive content and connecting customers and digital communications technology. He splits his time between New York City and East Hampton, New York, with his wife, Julie, and their dog, Toni.

Gabriella Cyranski has designed, managed, and executed physical, hybrid, and virtual event programs for over twenty years. At Intrado Digital Media, Gabriella works with clients to develop virtual event strategies that drive attendance and revenue and executive produces hybrid event television broadcasts that are syndicated globally. Gabriella's goal in life is to see the world. When she's not traversing the globe, she lives in Chicago with her husband, Eric, and their bull terriers, Bob, Peppa, and Siggy.

Appendix: Glossary of Terms

Artificial Intelligence (AI) involves having computers perform tasks that require human intelligence or decision making.

Audio Visual (A/V) equipment with both sound and visual components used for presentations, including screens, monitors, projectors, microphones, video, and sound equipment.

Augmented Reality (AR) the combination of the real world and virtual world that is integrated within a virtual environment. It takes things one step further than integrating a live video feed into a virtual environment by introducing computer-generated senses including sound, sight, touch, and smell.

Audio Engineer responsible for quality audio mix for onsite audiences and makes adjustments to audio mix per interviewer and video playback(s). He or she monitors microphone settings and controls volume of each speaker and ensures that everyone is "mic'd" correctly and on time.

Bumper (video bumper) short (usually 10 seconds or less) video clips at the beginning and end of the video that show the brand or company that your video represents.

Camera Operator sets up and controls all camera operation and functionality and takes cues from the director to make adjustments as needed.

Carbon Footprint total greenhouse gas emissions caused by an individual, event, organization, service, or product, expressed as carbon dioxide equivalent.

Certified Meeting Professional (CMP) recognized certification programs for professionals in the meeting, convention, and exhibition industries, organized by the Convention Industry Council.

Closeup Shot tightly frames the individual, making their reaction the main focus in the frame.

Concurrent Sessions shorter sessions which are scheduled to take place at the same time, each focusing on a different topic, usually within the same track.

Customer Testimonials company or product endorsements or recommendations from your strongest customer allies that affirm the value of a product or service.

Customer Relationship Management (CRM) a shared online database system that stores a major list of contacts and their details. This system allows companies to manage their interaction, event attendance history, and communications with their clients in an organized way.

Digital Event Strategist (DES) certification offered by Professional Convention Management Association (PCMA) that teaches an event professional how to strategically plan, produce, and measure digital and hybrid (in-person and digital) events.

Director in charge of the activities involved in making a video or television program or section of a program.

Emcee/MC the host who presides over the event program. *Emcee* is short for Master of Ceremonies.

Encoding Technician responsible for the configuration and monitoring of all live streaming equipment for every unique connection.

Environmental, Social, and Governance (ESG) refers to the three central factors in measuring the sustainability and societal impact of an investment in a company or business.

Executive Producer/Show Runner leads the production team and holds ultimate management and creative authority for the program and will be the main client contact.

Floor Manager responsible for giving information from the director in the control room, to the crew on the studio floor, and then back to the director.

Gamification a set of activities and processes to solve problems by using or applying the characteristics of game elements.

Graphics Operator configures the equipment that provides video and graphics playback during the program.

High Definition (HD) high-resolution video; generally any video image with considerably more than 480 vertical scan lines or 576 vertical lines is considered high-definition.

Hybrid Event is a physical event that has a portion or the entire content program available online.

Key Performance Indicator (KPI) a type of performance measurement. KPIs evaluate the success of an organization or of a particular activity in which it engages.

Keynote the opening address or important plenary session at a meeting that sets the tone or theme of the event.

Livestream coverage of an event broadcast live over the internet, often via social media channels.

Lower thirds a combination of text and graphical elements placed in the lower area of the screen to give the audience more information on who the speaker is.

Marketing automation platform (MAP) software platforms and technologies designed for marketing departments and organizations to more effectively market on multiple channels online and automate repetitive tasks.

Mid-shot frames the whole subject in your video shot from the waist up.

Moderator responsible for maintaining a consistent flow throughout the program, including making a general introduction of the webcast/content block, introducing each speaker, and running the live Q&A session.

On-Demand content available online that the viewer can access and watch whenever it is convenient.

Over the Top (OTT) named in reference to devices that go "over" a cable box to give the user access to TV content. In OTT channels, content is delivered via an internet connection rather than through a traditional cable/broadcast provider (think Roku or Apple TV).

Producer a person who oversees one or more aspects of video production on a television program. Producers all report up to the executive producer/show runner.

Production Assistant performs various production-related tasks as needed and is vital to setup and testing of the overall production.

Return on Investment (ROI) the ratio between the net profit made and the cost of investment in the production of an event.

Roving Reporter a professional host enables you to take your audience on a journey around the event space by conducting interviews with attendees, sponsors, and presenters directly from the show floor.

Run of Show a minute-by-minute sequence of events that will happen within the program.

Simu Live prerecorded sessions that are generally available to run at a specific time and date and are not publicized as being prerecorded and usually have a live post-presentation Q&A period.

Shot Setup the camera position and movement, lighting scheme, and anything else that physically must go on to capture the shot.

Smart TV a traditional television set with integrated internet and interactive web features which allows users to stream music and videos, browse the internet, and view photos.

Streaming a broadcast that is going to social media locations like Facebook Live, YouTube, Twitch, Periscope/Twitter, LinkedIn Live, OTT channels like Roku's Smart TV and Apple TV, or imbedded into a company's website or partner's website.

Syndication program broadcast simultaneously over a number of different communication channels (e.g. social channels, websites, mobile apps).

Technical Director responsible for video switcher deployment, configuration, and deployment.

Video Editor manages all pre- and post-production video editing needs during the event.

Virtual Reality (VR) a computer-generated artificial environment which you can experience by sight and sound and your actions can sometimes determine what happens next.

Webcam video camera that feeds or streams an image or video in real time through a computer.

Webcast an online broadcast that takes place at a specific date and time.

Webinar traditionally an audio-over-slide broadcast that includes Q&A and chat functionality.

Web conferencing a collaboration tool, it is a many-to-many solution – think of products like Zoom, WebEx, BlueJeans, Hoot, and a whole host of others.

INDEX